About me

I studied Drama, Applied Theatre and Education at the Royal Central School of Speech and Drama in London. I then worked as a freelance drama teacher for ten years, from Stagecoach academies in leafy suburbia to deprived schools in East London.
I worked for theatre companies, youth theatres, and state, private and special schools. In 2012 I set up my own youth theatre, which quickly grew into one of the largest regional youth theatres in the UK with over 250 students attending each week. And now I'd like to share everything I learned about being a freelance drama teacher with you.

TEACH DRAMA

How to Make a Living as a
Freelance Drama Teacher

Samantha Marsden

Published by Drama Fountain 2016

First published in Great Britain in 2016 by
Drama Fountain

Drama Fountain
86 Paul Street, London EC2A 4NE

www.dramafountain.com

ISBN 978-0-9957618-1-0

Typeset in Bembo Std

Printed and bound by CPI Group (UK) Ltd, Croydon, CR0 4YY

For actors and

drama practitioners who

wish to inspire.

Contents

Acknowledgements

I'm very grateful for the amount of support I've received for this book. Many thanks to Toby Marsden, Marianne Edwards, David Farmer, Adam Davenport, Helen Marshall, Debi Rush, Liz Hague, Sally Catlin, Holly Dabbs, Brian Conroy, Rhiannon Wallace, Lauren Senatore and Ellie Tillotson.

About David Farmer

David Farmer is a freelance writer, theatre director,
drama consultant and founder of the popular website
Drama Resource. After training as a primary school
teacher he founded Tiebreak Theatre Company, which
performed plays and workshops to over half a million
young people in schools, theatres and festivals across
the UK and abroad for a period of twenty-five years.
He runs courses in London and delivers training for
schools, arts organisations and language schools in
the UK and internationally.

Foreword

If you enjoy drama and working with children and
young people, then working as a freelance drama teacher
may be a natural career move. This book offers a great
deal of down-to-earth practical advice to those starting
out in the profession from someone who has proved her
worth in many different areas of the field – by teaching
in and running academies, schools and clubs and by man-
aging a very successful youth theatre.

The author takes the reader right through the process
from deciding which avenues to pursue, who to contact,
how much to charge and where to find work. The book
is full of solid-gold tips and advice covering interview
tips and techniques, lesson-planning, relationships with
clients and students, tips for maintaining discipline and
legal requirements. There is advice on choosing a show
to perform, how to schedule rehearsals and, last but not
least, a list of organisations to contact for training needs
and work opportunities. The interviews with freelancers
and professionals add an extra dimension and invaluable
advice from those in the know.

Reading this book will give anyone with the right mo-
tivation a head-start by offering advice about becoming
a highly-organised and effective freelance drama teacher from someone who has clearly demonstrated their
knowledge and success in the field.

—*David Farmer*

I never teach my pupils.

I only attempt to provide

the conditions in which

they can learn.

— *Albert Einstein*

ONE

Life as a Freelance Drama Teacher

Could *you* be a freelance drama teacher?

Maybe you're an actor, or you've just finished a degree in drama. Whether or not you have experience with children, if you have trained—or you're training—in drama, applied theatre or acting, then you *can* be a freelance drama teacher. All you need is an eagerness to learn, lesson ideas and some good classroom management techniques. I'll talk about these later in the book.

Why teach drama?

A well taught drama class gives students confidence, a
place to be creative and a platform to let off emotional
steam. A drama class is the place where even the most
angry, shy, or academically behind children can shine. I've
seen drama change lives over and over again.

What's it like to work as a freelance drama teacher?

At 4pm you might be pretending to be a gorilla with five
year olds, but two hours later you may be moved to tears
by a 16 year old delivering a touching monologue. Your
iPod will fill with the playlists you use in class, props will
live behind your sofa, and unlike some of your other actor friends who might be waitressing and taking telesales
jobs, you will look forward to going to work.

I love the lifestyle that comes from being a freelance
drama teacher. I adore the variety, the creativity and the
pressure. You will play drama games, improvise and direct
shows. There's nothing like watching a cast of children
perform something they're proud of. And that buzz after
the show—it's electric! But more about how to direct a
show later.

If you love drama, directing and children, then being
a freelance drama teacher is for you. However, a lot of
people want to, and not everyone makes it.

To make a living out of this highly rewarding and creative job, you need a killer CV, strong teaching tech-

niques and a good business mind. In this book I will teach you everything you need to know to be successful.

The pay

Most freelance drama teachers are paid £20 to £30 per teaching hour. You won't be paid for planning lessons, and you will be expected to stay behind for the occasional meeting, rehearsal and performance without pay.

You'll need to find 14 to 25 hours of teaching work per week during term time (32 to 36 weeks a year), plus three to six weeks' worth of school holiday workshops, in order to make a living.

The hours

It's likely that you'll be teaching after-school clubs in the afternoons, youth theatres in the evenings and weekend theatre schools, well, at the weekend! If you are serious about making a living as a freelance drama teacher, you *will* need to work some evenings and weekends. But, on the bright side, you will have time during the week for yourself. For the actor, this is a blessing as it's when auditions tend to be. Other plus sides to working evenings and weekends are that you'll travel during off-peak times, you can get an off-peak gym membership and if you're in a house-share, you get the place to yourself during the week. Unsociable work hours do have their advantages.

You won't be working unsociable hours all year round though, only during term time, which is about 32 to 36 weeks a year. For the other 10–14 weeks a year, during the school holidays, you'll be working sociable hours teaching theatre-themed holiday workshops. Or you *might* even take some time off.

Your clients

Your client is the person who pays you. The client is often the headmaster or mistress of the theatre school or the artistic director of the theatre company you're working for. Your client is your boss, but *not* your employer. Unless your client has set you up under the PAYE tax system (which is very unlikely), then they do not employ you. A freelance drama teacher is self-employed and provides the client with a service. But because you are not employed you don't get sick pay, guaranteed work or holiday pay. Being self-employed means you do your own tax return and you must register as self-employed with Her Majesty's Revenue and Customs (HMRC).

The work

There are many different types of work you can get. I recommend being as versatile as possible. Try to get experience teaching all age groups and don't be a snob about what type of work you take on. Some teachers turn their nose up at directing something like *Annie*, but if you want to make a living as a freelance drama teacher then you need to be willing to do what your client wants, even if it's not quite to your tastes. Let's take a look at the different types of clients you may work for.

Franchised children's theatre schools

Stagecoach, Razzamataz, The Pauline Quirke Academy… the list goes on. These places are a fabulous source of income for the freelance drama teacher. I worked for Stagecoach for eight years and they were an amazing company to work for. They pay well, treat their staff with respect and give you a fair amount of creative freedom. I worked for Stagecoach in Wimbledon, Chiswick, Highgate and Swindon. Every Stagecoach is slightly different, but I had a wonderful experience at all of them. At one point I earned a full time income by working for Stagecoach on Friday evenings, all day on Saturdays and on Sunday mornings. Go to the directory in the back of this book for a full list of franchised children's theatre schools in the UK to contact: these companies are always on the lookout for enthusiastic teachers.

Youth theatres and privately owned drama groups

Most towns and cities will have their own youth theatre, plus several other drama groups run privately by individuals. Often these run during evenings and weekends in school halls, church halls, arts spaces and theatres.

Teaching abroad

Lately more and more drama teaching jobs are coming up abroad, particularly in China. These contracts tend to last for anything from two to twelve months. Often you will have your flights and board paid for, plus you will be paid a little pocket money. Great work for those who want to travel. These jobs are often advertised on online job boards.

After-school clubs

There's two ways you can do this one. You can work for an existing company that runs after-school clubs. Or you can set up your own club. If you work for someone else they'll do all the legwork and you'll get £20 to £40 for teaching an after-school club, which is normally one hour to 90 minutes in length. Alternatively you can set up your own after-school club and earn £50 to £90 per session. I'll show you how to set up your own club in chapter eight.

Special needs schools

Special needs schools get funding for specialised teachers and facilitators to come in and provide workshops. Contact all the special needs schools within travelling distance and offer them a drama workshop. If they like you, you may get invited back on a weekly basis. I worked in several special needs schools, providing one-hour weekly drama workshops. To start with I felt like an imposter, as I wasn't trained to work with students with special needs. However some special schools have visiting musicians and artists who don't have this specific training. As a freelance drama teacher you will never be left alone with students, and there will always be at least two or three trained members of staff in the room with you. The highlight of my teaching career was when a nine-year-old non-verbal autistic boy spoke for the first time ever in my drama class. People who studied drama at university or drama school tend to be naturally good with people with special needs as confidence and the ability to have fun are essential. Think *Mr Tumble*.

Here are a few tips for working with people with special needs:

- React to the students' needs and be flexible

- Treat the students with respect

- Be confident

- Keep your lessons simple and visually stimulating

- Bring plenty of props, music and enthusiasm

- Don't be patronising

- Sing

- Be yourself

- If you can, learn a little bit of sign language.

Working in Private Schools

Private schools sometimes have the budget to take on a freelance drama teacher, so it is worth approaching them. They may want you to come in and do a one day workshop on a particular theme: Shakespeare, improv, voice, Roald Dahl, etc. Or they may want you on a more regular basis, maybe to run an after-school club or to help out with an overstretched drama department. I worked for a top private school in Bath for several years, running two after-school clubs and doing freelance directing projects for them.

Freelance directing is good fun, although slightly stressful! For freelance directing I charge per show. You can charge anything between £800 and £2000 for a show. To put on a show you'll need a minimum of two 90-minute sessions every week for ten weeks and then two full days of rehearsals just before the performance.

Another option that private schools like is the 'play in a week'. You can charge anything between £500 and £1400 for the week. This may sound like a lot of money to charge for just one week's work, but you'll spend two weeks working. One week planning the show and the second week rehearsing the show with students.

Putting on a play in a week is both stressful *and* highly rewarding!

State schools

In my experience it's harder to get work in state schools than private schools, as they tend to have less money to spend. However, I have been asked to do one-off work-shops in state schools, both primary and secondary. One secondary school I worked for liked to get me in during the lead up to GCSE and A level practical drama exams; I'd help the students with their practical exam pieces. You can write directly to secondary schools offering this service.

Primary schools sometimes like drama workshops too, particularly if you can offer drama workshops that pro-mote literacy. For a one day workshop you can charge anything between £80 and £500. Personally I think £120-160 is about right.

LAMDA teaching

Some people make a full time living out of teaching LAMDA. You get paid less per hour than you would for group teaching. But if teaching large groups isn't your thing, and you prefer doing one-to-one tuition, then LAMDA teaching might be for you. On average you get paid between £10 and £30 per hour to teach LAMDA.

Many of the weekend theatre schools like Stagecoach offer LAMDA to their students, and they are often look-ing for LAMDA teachers. Private schools are also often keen to take on freelance LAMDA teachers. You can also set yourself up as a private LAMDA tutor and hire out a space so the students come directly to you. It's easy to register. Here's what LAMDA say on their website:

> You do not require any specific training or qualifications in order to teach learners and prepare them for LAMDA examinations. Similarly, we don't dictate how you approach the teaching, how often you see the learners or in what format you conduct your classes. All the subject requirements are detailed in the individual syllabuses which you can download or purchase online, but we leave the specific teaching approach and timeline up to you and your learners!
>
> We also have a Directory of LAMDA Teachers which represents a list of those wishing to advertise the fact that they are preparing learners for LAMDA examinations. Please note, they are not employed by LAMDA and are therefore not endorsed by us either. If you would like to join the Directory, please visit the Store and purchase a Membership.

Theatre companies

Very few theatre companies offer work to freelance drama teachers. Nevertheless, do send them your CV as very occasionally positions do come up.

Government funded projects

Sometimes the government or charities offer funding for drama projects. Very occasionally there are grants and funding opportunities that freelance drama teachers can apply for. However, sadly, with cuts in arts funding these opportunities are getting fewer and fewer. And they were rare to start with.

Theatre in Education

There are various Theatre in Education companies who take performers/teachers on. But this is a different job from that of a freelance drama teacher. It's suited to performers who like to travel and don't mind devoting their entire time to a short term contract. Although it can be great fun, TIE is not an area I cover in this book.

THE INTERVIEW

Adam Davenport, Creative Director at The Pauline Quirke Academy of Performing Arts

What do you like to see in a covering letter?

I like to see evidence that the covering letter has been thought about, and is personal to the Pauline Quirke Academy, and to the position advertised. I have received so many letters from people who haven't taken a few minutes to find out who to address the application to, and on many occasions, the name of our company is spelled incorrectly! Once I received a letter detailing why they would like to work at a different performing arts organisation – it was clearly a template and they'd forgotten to change the names.

Apart from the above, I love to see a genuine enthusiasm and passion for teaching, and an explanation as to why they feel they are suitable for the role and what they can they bring. Two to three paragraphs are often sufficient.

How can someone impress you in an interview?

I am always impressed when a candidate has done their research on the company, and can talk confidently about our creative structure, demonstrating an understanding of what is required from our acting teachers. Somebody who is intelligent, articulate and experienced, but is fun, down to earth and doesn't take themselves too seriously. Somebody who I think would be a role model for the students.

What do you think makes a good teacher?

Somebody who is genuinely passionate about working with children. Not only developing them as performers, but as individuals. Understanding the ethos that every student has something to offer. It's our job as teachers to find out what that is, and show students that they are valued, encouraging growth and confidence. A good teacher is well prepared, and always looking for exciting and innovative ways to explore actor training. They keep lessons inspiring, introducing as many varied elements of acting as possible, such as mask work, devising, phys-ical theatre, and commedia dell'arte, keeping students hooked. Not to mention different performing opportunities like promenade, in-the-round etc. I love to see a teacher who is charismatic and fun, yet can hold attention and instil respect, discipline and performance etiquette.

What advice would you give to someone who wants to be a freelance drama teacher?

Watch and read as many plays as possible. Keep your knowledge fresh and up to date by attending classes at institutions such as The Actors Centre. If you have no teaching experience, contact your local weekend perform-ing arts academies or vocational institutions, and ask if you can shadow a teacher for work experience. Accept one-off cover or 'dep' sessions to add to your CV. Keep an eye on fantastic websites such as *artsjobs.org.uk* for the latest teaching vacancies. Ensure you plan your lessons well in order to deliver high quality sessions, and build a reputation for excellence. Word soon gets around and you will start to get booked frequently! Above all, be positive, exciting and passionate; enjoy watching students trans-form as they build their confidence and acting technique.

Leap and the

net will appear.

— *John Burroughs*

TWO
Getting Started

The first step to getting started is to give your CV a makeover. Part of my job as artistic director at Chippenham Youth Theatre was to read the many covering letters and CVs that were sent to me. If your CV can meet the criteria I've listed below, it will put you in the top 20% of applicants. Even if you don't have very much teaching experience, you are likely to be taken more seriously.

What to include in your CV

- Tailor the CV to the role. If you're an actor, don't send your acting CV. Instead, edit the CV so that it's suitable for a teaching application

- Presentation is key. Make sure it's clearly laid out and simple to follow

- Keep the CV to two A4 pages, maximum

- Keep it updated

- Include a summary sentence at the top of your CV saying what you do. Mine reads: *Freelance drama teacher for 3-18 year olds—mainstream and with special needs—and drama, singing and dance teacher for 3-7 year olds*

- If you have a criminal records check from the government Disclosure and Barring Service (DBS), say so

- Remember to include your contact details

- If you don't have enough drama teaching experience on your CV, include a short paragraph describing your teaching style

- Include two quotes outlining what someone has said about your teaching or relevant work. Ask an old employer, client or teacher for the quotes. You'll be amazed at the lovely things they'll say about you!

Mine are:

'Sam had such a positive and inclusive attitude towards our pupils. During her sessions she was able to energise and enthuse even our most hard to reach children.'
Gemma Baker, Head, Side by Side Special School

'An outstanding and enchanting teacher. A lovely enthusiastic energy to the class. Sam has an excellent approach to discipline.'
External Stagecoach inspector

How to write a cover letter (or cover email)

- Address the cover letter to a named person wherever possible and avoid Sir/Madam

- Offer to teach a taster class for free so that they can see you in action

- Keep it short – five to six sentences

- Summarise your relevant experience in one or two sentences

- Say where and what you studied

- Avoid talking about what you need and focus on what the potential client needs. For example don't say things like, 'It's my dream to...', 'I'm looking to get experience in...' and 'I was hoping you might be able to help me.' Instead, talk about how your experience will meet the demands of the company.

Do talk about how you can help them. For example, 'I have experience working with 7-11 year olds and an up to date criminal records check,' or 'if you ever need a volunteer please don't hesitate to contact me'

- Make sure there are no grammar, punctuation, or spelling errors. Some people apologise for errors in their covering letter saying they are dyslexic. I sympathise with this, as I am dyslexic. However many potential clients will *not* sympathise and will write you off as unprofessional. If you are dyslexic get your covering letter and CV proof-read.

What to do if you have no teaching experience

Getting that first teaching job can be hard. It's unlikely that someone will give you work unless you have experience. But how do you get teaching experience if no one will *give* you teaching experience? Here are some options.

A friend, or a friend of a friend

The easiest way to get your first gig is to get it through someone you know. Ask friends, friends of friends, drama teachers, old drama teachers, the guy who serves coffee at the theatre bar you go to regularly. Ask everyone you have some kind of connection to.

Your previous drama teacher is a particularly great person to ask. That's how I got my first teaching job. When I was 18, I gave the director of my old youth theatre a call, even though I hadn't spoken to him for four years. I told him I wanted to teach drama and the following week he invited me in for a trial class to teach the 12-14 year olds (notoriously the hardest age group to teach!). It went badly, I thought, but he offered me a job and I became their teacher. That position opened many other doors for me. Being able to earn £25 an hour from the age of 18 allowed me to do many things I wouldn't have been able to do otherwise.

Ten years later, when I was running my own Youth theatre, I was always keen to give old students teaching opportunities. I wanted to see them succeed, after all who doesn't want to see their old students do well? Contact all your old drama teachers, even if you haven't spoken to them in years; they'll be pleased to hear from you and keen to help.

Become a teaching assistant

If you have no experience with children, becoming a teaching assistant (TA) is a good option. You can write to the companies in the directory at the back of this book offering them your services. They may well be very keen to hear from you as 95% of the CVs they receive will be from people looking for teaching work and not TA work. The experience is likely to pay off later when you're looking for a job as a teacher. You may even be promoted from TA to teacher if the teacher you are assisting leaves.

It is also possible to get TA work via an agency that provides TAs to schools. When I was starting out in London,

I worked for the agency Classroom. They found me TA
jobs in different special needs schools. They were lovely
to work for and very flexible. They were friendly, always
had work when I wanted it (even if I didn't work for
them for a few months) and they paid weekly. This agency love taking actors and drama students, so if you're in
London and you're looking for experience with children,
or a little extra income, do contact them.

Classroom Teachers
Langham House
308 Regent Street
London
W1B 3AT

Email: enquiries@classroomteachers.co.uk
Phone: 020 7636 0600

There are also many other teaching assistant agencies in
and outside of London.

Take a short course

Taking a short teaching course will look good on your
CV and may help you get your first job. Many potential
clients run courses that you can attend. By taking a short
course you may make useful contacts, you'll improve
your CV and you will learn new skills to become a
better teacher. Even if you've been teaching for years it's
good to take a course now and then to freshen up your
skills. Check out the short courses list in the back of this
book.

What to do if you have experience but you'd like more work

If you are a freelance drama teacher and you have some teaching work but not enough, there are a few things you can do:

- Be willing to travel further

- Contact private schools

- Contact special needs schools

- Set up an after-school club

- Improve your CV and covering letter

- Evaluate your lessons. Make sure they are engaging and that your students and clients are happy with your work.

'Dep' sessions

You may get asked to do a 'dep' session. This means a cover lesson. You may get a phone call from a company at very short notice asking you to come in and teach, as their regular teacher has just phoned in sick, or has an audition. Do your best to accept their offer, as this work can often lead to a permanent position. You can also include dep work on your CV.

Searching for a listed job

It's a good idea to check out job listings once a week. However many companies don't advertise positions because they already have a stack of CVs to choose from. Therefore, I strongly recommend that you send out your CV to companies even if they are not recruiting. Here are some of the best websites that list freelance drama teaching work:

- *www.dramaclasses.biz/drama-teachers-wanted*

- *www.artsjobs.org.uk*

- *www.thestage.co.uk/jobs/categories/teaching-education*

- *ccskills.org.uk/careers/jobs*

Write to Everyone

Send your covering letter and CV to every place you are willing to travel to for work. Go through the directory in the back of this book and look up drama groups local to your area. After you've sent your CV out you may not hear anything back, but then six months or even a year later, you could get a phone call. I recently got a job offer from a CV I sent to a drama company over five years ago!

Where you live makes a difference

London

Central London (Zones 1 to 3) is the hardest place to find work. It's very competitive because there are many incredibly talented teachers and actors, but not very many children.

Outer London areas

This is a good place to find work. There are lots of children and many drama companies. It is still competitive though, as the capital is a magnet for drama school graduates and actors. Places like Wimbledon, Muswell HIll, Kingston, and Croydon have lots of opportunities for the freelance drama teacher.

Cities

Cities outside London are the easiest place to find work. Bristol, Manchester, Reading, and other major towns and cities don't have as much competition for work, and many children live in these areas. When I moved out of London to Bath, I was shocked by how much work was available. In and around Bath there aren't many freelance drama teachers, but lots of children. I was treated like royalty—it was great!

Small towns and the countryside

You are unlikely to find much pre-existing work in these areas although you may find the occasional youth theatre. In places where there's not much going on I recommend you start up your own after-school drama clubs and drama groups. You will find there is a high demand for them as there are lots of children in small towns and rural areas, but not so much for them to do.

THE INTERVIEW

Helen Marshall, Freelance Drama Teacher

BA Hons in Performing Arts from The University of Cumbria (formerly Cumbria Institute of the Arts), First Class.

Which companies have you worked for as a freelance drama teacher?

Bigfoot, London – Covering teachers' Planning, Preparation and Assessment (PPA) time as an arts specialist.

Which companies do you currently work for as a freelance drama teacher?

West Yorkshire Playhouse, Freshwater Theatre Company, Allotment Theatre Company and I run and manage Theatre Tots Ltd Manchester.

How did you get your first job as a freelance drama teacher?

I started working for a teaching agency as a teaching assistant, and gained some experience in primary schools. Then I worked at a summer camp teaching drama, which I loved. I continued to work for them when they needed staff in the holidays. From there I worked up to drama leader. Then I saw an advertisement for a drama facilitator job on Arts Jobs for Theatre Tots. I realised I could teach through my performance skills, and it didn't always have to be in a school setting! Theatre Tots gave me the confidence to go for other drama facilitator jobs.

What advice would you give to someone who wants to be a freelance drama teacher?

- Be patient
- Be flexible
- Continue to grow and train
- Stay organised.

What's your favourite drama game?

It's so simple and one I nearly always begin with: Stop/Go. It breaks the ice and allows a group to instantly relax, laugh at themselves, work together, focus, concentrate and think about spatial awareness. You can link the Stop/Go game to whichever topic you are teaching.

What's your teaching philosophy in a nutshell?

I am passionate about using drama as an educational tool, as it allows us to imagine, express, and question, which in my opinion helps children understand, motivating them to learn about the world around them.

Be yourself;

everyone else is

already taken.

— *Oscar Wilde*

THREE

The Interview

So you've been asked in for an interview. Yay! Most companies will want to interview you, plus they'll want to see you in action, teaching a class. I'll cover both in this chapter.

What to wear?

You should wear what you'd wear if you were going to teach a drama class. You want the interviewer to be able to imagine you as a drama teacher, which may be difficult for them if you turn up in a suit and tie. Wear something that you can move about in, but also make sure it is reasonably smart. Many headmasters and head-mistresses hate teachers wearing jeans, so it's best to avoid them. Wear comfy shoes, no heels or boots. Jazz shoes or dance trainers are a good choice. Make sure to keep your hair off your face: your face, after all, is one of your most important tools as a drama teacher. Try not to smoke just before the interview, but if you must, wash your hands and have a mint so that you don't smell of cigarettes.

Research

Before the interview, make sure to have researched the company. Find out what they do and, most importantly, what their teaching ethos is. The more you know about them, the more they'll be impressed. If you can refer-ence some of this research during the interview, then top marks to you. For example, 'I saw the photos of your production of Romeo and Juliet on your website, it looked amazing.' Then if you can link that back to your experience even better, 'I directed a scene from Romeo and Juliet at University. I have a passion for Shakespeare.'

Arrival time

Never arrive late or flustered from being in rush. Try to arrive ten minutes early.

What to bring

- A copy of your CV

- A portfolio if you have one, with pictures from shows you've been in, or directed. This isn't necessary, but it can be impressive

- If you *really* want to impress, go all out and take an example of your lesson plans.

Be authentic

Be yourself in the interview, they want to get to know you and see who you are. Confidence, authenticity, positivity and focus are key.

Good body language

If you've studied drama you'll know all about this. Maintain good body language in the interview, even if you're nervous. Avoid slouching, playing with a pen, looking into the distance, fidgeting, playing with your hair, touching your face, and touching the interviewer. Remember to smile, make eye contact, sit up straight, listen actively and nod.

Sell yourself

Talk about your achievements and bring up examples that demonstrate your experience throughout the interview. Don't be shy about repeatedly explaining why you are perfect for the job.

Know your stuff

Make sure you have an idea about your teaching philosophy, your approach to discipline, and what kind of content you'll deliver in your lessons.

Say 'Thank you'

Thank the interviewer for their time at the end of the interview and if it feels right say something complimentary about the company.

Practise responses

Practise responses to questions you might be asked. Don't learn your response word for word, as you don't want to *sound* practised, but have an idea of how you'll respond to questions. Don't make the answers too short: the interviewer wants to hear your answers. Remember it's *you* that's meant to be doing most of the talking and not the interviewer. Below are some potential questions you might be asked.

- So, can you tell me about yourself?

- What would an outstanding drama lesson look like to you?

- Why do you think teaching drama is important?

- Let's say, for example, you have a child in your class who doesn't want to join in, how would you deal with that?

- How would someone else describe you as a teacher?

- Why do you want to teach drama?

- Why do you want to work for our school/theatre company?

- What was your experience at drama school or university?

- There may be a question related to your CV, for example, 'your CV says you taught drama in China last year, can you tell me about that?'

- If you were to direct our students in a show, what show might you choose?

- Do you have any experience directing?

- What are your strengths?

- What are your weaknesses?

- Where would you like to be five years from now?

- What did you like least about your last job?

- Do you have any questions for us?

- Can you give me an example of a time you went above and beyond the call of duty at work?

- How would you handle a disruptive student?

- What would you like students to get from your drama lessons?

- How would you describe your teaching style?

- What are you most proud of?

- What are the qualities of a good teacher?

Teaching as part of the interview

Most companies will ask you to teach as part of the interview. Very often people become a different person when they teach. I've interviewed the most wonderful potential teachers with great answers to my questions, and who were enthusiastic and well presented. They've got the job, I tell myself. But then I put them in front of a class and they turn into the frightening Miss Trunchbull! And I am shocked as they are nothing like the lovely person I just interviewed.

Some people turn into a different person when they teach: crazed, aggressive and frankly quite scary! There really is no need to take on a different character when you teach. You should be your best, relaxed self. Be kind, be firm and most importantly be authentic. It is authenticity that will give you a good rapport with the students.

And it's a good rapport with the students that the interviewer is looking for during the trial class.

The trial class normally happens in one of three ways. You may be asked to:

- Teach a full-length class to the potential class you would be teaching if you got the job

- Teach a group of children for a short period of time: 10, 20 or 30 minutes

- Teach the fellow adult interviewees and pretend they are your students. You'll be expected to participate in their class too.

The third option is the scariest and becoming more common. If you are asked to teach fellow interviewees my advice is to pretend that they are children. Stay animated, enthusiastic and uninhibited. The adult interviewees will probably have a lower energy than a group of children would, but don't let that bring your energy down.

However if your trial class consists of teaching a class of children, this comes with other problems. When children, or teenagers, first meet a teacher, they like to test the rules, and test the teacher. Just what you *don't* need when you have the headmistress or headmaster of the school sat there taking notes on your teaching style. But don't worry, all the other applicants will have this problem too.

If you act unconfidently, or let the students dictate the rules, you will get yourself into trouble quickly, which may cost you the job. Confidence is key. Even if you're terrified, act confident. You must behave like a leader if you want the students to treat you as one. Hold your head up high, believe in your lesson plan, and don't accept any misbehaving. It's OK to tell students off in your trial class.

At the start of any class, you should spend one to two minutes laying out your rules. Children and teenagers like boundaries, and they like you to enforce them. You can read more about this in chapter six, Classroom Discipline. You also want the students to like you, so make sure to be fair with your rules and to treat the students with respect, always thinking the best in them. Make sure your trial class is fun and that you do some 'real acting' (as they would call it) and not just drama games.

Trial class lesson content

Include your favourite games and acting exercises. If you love the activities you're doing, so will your students, and so will the person watching and considering you for the job.

Learn your lesson plan off by heart. It's off-putting to see a teacher fumbling with a piece of paper, plus it makes them look less confident. You don't need to make the lesson content too original or complicated. Traditional drama activities are fine; the interviewer is probably more interested in your teaching style rather than the lesson content.

Top tips

- Get the students to like you. Turn on the charisma, be inspiring, be fair, smile, respect them, maintain good classroom discipline, and make sure your lesson content is fun and interesting

- Tailor the lesson content for the age of the group

- Stay focused on your students. Don't glance over to the interviewer, to your lesson plan or anyone walking past your classroom

- Stay in control. You are the teacher, not the students or the person watching you teach

- Stay calm

- Don't rush. You may be eager to show off the great variety of drama games you know. But it's better to showcase one exercise well than do three badly

- For the trial lesson forget about learning the students' names. You don't have time and it will distract from your lesson content

- Own that space. You are the teacher and it's your space. If you want the chairs put to the side of the room, don't be afraid to ask the class to help you do to it. If you want the window open, lights on, bags and coats somewhere else, do it. There's no need to ask permission. The interviewer will be pleased you're using common sense and that you're taking charge

- Do a quick safety check of the room, and if you see something dangerous warn the class before you begin your lesson, for example, 'please can everyone stay away from the chairs, they're stacked high and could topple down.' The interviewer will be really happy that you have thought about keeping your students safe.

THE INTERVIEW

Debi Rush, Company Director at Little Tanks

What do you like to see in a covering letter?

Details about their:
- Experience
- Knowledge
- Training
- Techniques
- Availability
- Enthusiasm.

How can someone impress you in an interview?

I like people to be punctual and enthusiastic, and to be knowledgeable about my company. Also it's good to be relaxed, interactive and informative about communicating experience relevant to the role.

What do you think makes a good teacher?

- Being flexible
- Reliable
- Have a good idea of class management and behaviour management techniques
- Able to plan, but also think on the spot
- Reflective on sessions, and act on any areas that need developing
- Creative
- Fun/cheery
- Ensure children are happy at all times

- Able to communicate with pupils, parents, employers and staff on site
- Able to build a good rapport with pupils
- Organised
- Have a flair for the arts
- Take on board ideas, as well as bringing own ideas to the groups
- Personable
- Knowledgeable about the pupils' era
- Take constructive criticism, and work on developing and areas that may need attention
- Excellent communication skills.

What advice would you give to someone who wants to be a freelance drama teacher?

- Be prepared to be flexible as well as organised
- Ensure you have the correct documents, and be willing to work with the person contracting you to ensure all is in place before starting work
- Do some research into companies before the interview, and check job descriptions carefully before committing to a contract
- Be honest and available for your client – especially if you are a jobbing actor
- Be prepared for some training, and for taking on policies and procedures of different companies.

Share your knowledge.

It is a way to achieve

immortality.

— *The 14th Dalai Lama*

FOUR

Lesson Plans

Your client may tell you what to teach. They may even give you lesson plans. However, this type of client is rare and normally you'll be expected to create your own lesson content.

I strongly recommend that you don't come to a class with a lesson plan that consists only of drama games, or even worse with no lesson plan at all. Although drama games are great, do be careful not to play drama games for your whole lesson.

The games and exercises you learned at drama school, or university, will come in very handy when planning your lessons. Share what you know on the subject, even if it is advanced. Make sure students learn something new in your lessons, and make the content challenging so as to keep their attention.

There are many great books and resources out there listing games and exercises. Here are some of my favourites.

- Book: *101 Drama Games and Activities* by David Farmer.

- Book: *Drama Games for Classrooms and Workshops* by Jessica Swale.

- Website: *Drama Resource*, *dramaresource.com/drama-games*

- YouTube channel: *Drama Menu*, *youtube.com/channel/UChFbmxYZ8VVThe_mcD1vo_A*

It's also great to get students working with scripts. Good sources of material include *The Railway Children, Little Red Riding Hood, Oliver Twist, A Little Princess, Wind and the Willows, Little Women, Snow White, The Wonderful Wizard of Oz, The Secret Garden, Animal Farm, Jane Eyre, Great Expectations* and *Pride and Prejudice*. Thirty-five different short scenes, for all ages, are included in my silver package, available on my website at *www.dramafountain.com*.

Example lesson plans

Here are some examples of my lesson plans, for three different age groups.

Example lesson plan: jungle-themed drama workshop, one hour, 3-7 year olds

- *10 minutes.* Register, news sharing and then explain what you'll be doing in class. Do a recap of rules if you have any new students

- *5 minutes.* Hello game. Go round the circle and each child gets to say whether they would like a shout, whisper or roar as their hello. If they say shout then the whole class shout, 'HELLO EMMA!' and if the next child sat in the circle says 'whisper,' the whole class whisper, 'Hello Amir.'

- *10 minutes.* Move around the room as different animals from the jungle. You call out the animal names and the children become the animals. After about five minutes ask the children to sit down and ask if anybody would like to show their animal to the class. One by one, let the volunteers show their animal and give each student a big round of applause if they do. Don't force anyone to show if they don't want to.

- *10 minutes.* Sing some jungle songs with actions. You can even ask the children to invent some of their own actions. If you don't know any jungle songs you can look some up on YouTube.

- *10 minutes.* Go on a safari. This age group love to go on an imaginary journey. Tell them you will now take them to the jungle, ask them to pack their bags, putting sun cream, sun hats, mosquito spray and so on into their bags. Then take them to the airport asking them to queue and check their passports. Get into character as an air hostess giving out aeroplane safety instructions and then drinks. Land. Ask everyone to put their sun cream on. Turn yourself into a jungle exploration leader. (I find an Australian accent works best!) Guide students through the jungle, pointing out animals and plants. One at a time students can become an animal and all of the jungle explorers can take photos of that animal. You can pick bananas and eat them, feed a monkey, be afraid of a tiger. The more you believe it and play it up the better! Make sure to finish the journey by getting back on the plane and landing in England.

- *10 minutes.* Monkey, Monkey, Snake. This is like Duck, Duck, Goose, but the words have been changed to a jungle theme. The children sit in a circle. One person walks around the circle tapping everyone on the head saying 'monkey, monkey, monkey, monkey…' but when they tap someone on the head and say 'snake' that person stands up and chases them around the circle and the person who tapped them has to sit down in their place. Now the person who was chasing taps people on the heads saying 'monkey, monkey…' Make sure everyone gets a turn.

- *5 minutes.* Ask students to put their hand up and share their favourite part of the lesson.

Example lesson plan: Drama workshop, 90 minutes, 7 - 11 year olds

- *10 minutes.* Register, news sharing and then explain what you'll be doing in class. Do a recap of rules if you have any new students.

- *5 minutes.* Stop/Go. When you say 'stop,' everyone walks around the space. When you say 'go', everyone stops. After you've played around with this, add some more actions decided on by the students. For example, 'sit on the floor' when you say 'jump' and 'jump' when you say 'sit on the floor.'

- *10 minutes.* 'Sausages.' Ask everybody to sit as an audience facing one chair centre stage. The person who sits on this chair is not allowed to smile. Students ask this person questions and the only answer they are allowed to give is 'sausages.' If the student sat on the chair smiles, they are out. Students can ask anything they like, for example,
'What do you brush your teeth with?'
'Sausages,' the straight faced person on the chair will reply.

- *10 minutes.* 'I'm sorry I…' Ask the class to sit in a circle and show a few examples of how this is played. The person stood in the middle of the circle has to go up to someone sat in the circle and apologise for something. The person apologising can make the apology as crazy as they like. Maybe they are a witch apologising that they turned someone's little brother into a pig, or perhaps they're a school teacher apologising because an exam won't be taking place today because of a flood, or maybe they're a friend saying sorry because they dropped their friend's iPhone down the toilet! The person being apologised to can react however the like: they might be angry, pleased or devastated.

- *10 minutes.* Creating characters. Ask students to walk around as different characters from fairytales. Thinking about posture, speed, facial expressions, mannerisms, quirks and so on. Tell them it doesn't matter if it's a girl or boy character – in drama, boys can play girls and girls can play boys. Once you've called out a dozen or so characters and they've acted these out, do the same thing again, but this time ask them to put a twist in their character. For example, maybe Little Red Riding Hood is a world famous rapper, or the wolf is a figure skater. Call out the fairytale characters again and enjoy watching them re-imagined. Then sit the students down and ask if anybody would like to show. One at a time, let students briefly show their character. Never force people to show, but do encourage the more reluctant students and make it a safe space by accepting and encouraging all the ideas, no matter how crazy!

- *20 minutes.* Group improvisation. Put students into groups of four or five and ask them to reimagine a fairytale and create a short, three to five minute improvisation of it. Give them some examples of re-imaginings: what if Cinderella were a poet who really disliked the snobbish prince and she fell in love with the coachman? What if the wolf was very lonely and all he wanted was to be friends with the three little pigs. Tell the students to keep it short and simple, and that a narrator might be a useful thing to include.

- *20 minutes.* Show all of the pieces. Ask students to give positive feedback. Leave the constructive criticism to the teacher to provide, as you need to be very careful not to block your students' creativity. You *do* want to give them a little constructive criticism so that they know how to improve next time.

- *5 minutes.* Ask students to put their hand up and share their favourite part of the lesson.

Example lesson Plan: Drama workshop, 90 minutes, 12-21 year olds

- *5 minutes.* Hello, register and explain what you'll be doing in class. A recap of the rules if you have any new students.

- *5 minutes.* 'Yes, Let's.' Ask students to stand in a space in the room, then initiate an action by saying 'Let's bake a cake.' Ask the class to reply with 'Yes, let's!' and then they all pretend to bake a cake. Then the students can shout out any idea they like, nothing is

too crazy.
'Let's wash a lion!'
'Yes, let's!'

- *10 minutes.* Walk round the room at different speeds.
  One being the slowest, ten being the fastest. Call out
  a variety of numbers and watch students walk around
  at different tempos. Then ask the class to put characters to these different speeds, for example number
  nine might be a businesswoman in a rush, whereas
  number two might be a surf dude on the beach.

- *20 minutes.* Sit down and talk about the difference
  between what a character says and what they are
  thinking. For example, when someone says they're
  'fine!' but their tone and delivery of the word tells
  you they are not. Place a chair centre-stage. The actor
  sitting on this chair will have an imaginary problem,
  it's important to tell the students that this must be an
  imaginary problem. Not a problem they are experi-
  encing in real life. Examples of problems the character can have include: they are being bullied at school,
  their parents are going through a divorce, or that
  their dog has died. The person on the chair is trying
  to hide their problem from the audience, however,
  they *can* let it affect them. The audience ask the actor
  questions, and it's the audience's job to find out what
  the problem is. The audience might ask about the
  person's home life, school and friends, and they will
  be able to tell by the actor's body language when
  they are getting close to the problem. They might
  ask, 'Do you have many friends at school?' and the

actor may look sad and shrug their shoulders saying, 'Kind of…' Then someone might say, 'Are you being bullied at school?' and the actor may say, 'Yes,' or 'I don't want to talk about it.' Don't do this activity with students under 12 and be careful to emphasise that this is acting, not real life. I have seen many of the best acting performances of my teaching life with this activity.

- *15 minutes.* Hand out a script to everyone (the same script, preferably one A4 page long.) I have included many different scripts for this activity in my silver package, but you can source your own. The best scripts for this activity will feature two to three characters. Ask students to give the character they are playing an underlying problem that is not verbally expressed in the script. Then ask them to rehearse this. The problem might be serious—they just found out their grandmother died—or funny: they need the toilet.

- *20 minutes.* Ask the students to perform and then share with the group the underlying problem they were playing.

- *10 minutes.* Park Bench. Two characters sit on a bench. One character has to try to get the other off the bench but without any physical contact. For example one person might be sat reading their newspaper and the other sits beside them and says, 'Oh my goodness, have you heard about the terrible storm that's going to hit the park?'

- *5 minutes.* Ask students what they thought of the lesson, how could it have been improved, and if it was useful to them.

Themed lessons

Sometimes it's good to have a theme for your lessons. Here are some ideas for students aged seven and over:

- Circus skills

- Stage fighting

- Acting for camera

- Shakespeare

- The Meisner technique

- Physical theatre

- Voice

- The Alexander Technique

- Directing

- Mask work

- Mime

- Comedy

- Musical theatre

- Poetry

- Melodrama

- Audition technique

- Devising

- Murder mystery

- Movement

- Commedia dell'arte.

For 3 - 7 year olds

With this age group, you need to keep your lessons fast-paced, simple, energetic and more games-based than you would for older students. This age group love themed lessons and there are many drama games that are easily adapted to fit into themes.

- Jungle

- Pirates

- Princes and princesses

- Fairy tales

- A workshop based on a popular book or film

- Circus skills

- Musical theatre

- Mask work

- Mime

- Poetry

- Witches and wizards

- Superheroes

- Spies.

THE INTERVIEW

Liz Hague, Storyteller, Freelance Drama Facilitator and Artistic Director at The Story Cellar

Drama & Theatre Studies with English at University College Chester.

Which companies do you currently work for as a freelance drama teacher?

I moved to Bristol in 2011 to start a family. I freelance for Bristol Old Vic, Travelling Light and The Tobacco Factory. I set up The Adult Company for the Bristol Old Vic with John Retallack to run alongside their young company. Then in January 2015 I set up The Story Cellar to run my own school workshops and community projects, most recently as resident storyteller at The Bristol Old Vic in school holidays. Please see the website for further information on the company and ways of practice.

www.thestorycellar.co.uk

Which companies have you worked for as a freelance drama teacher in the past?

Before moving to Bristol I worked as a freelance workshop facilitator in London for ten years. I worked for MakeBelieve Arts, Eastside Education, Half Moon Young People's Theatre, Shakespeare Schools Festival, Central School of Speech & Drama, Freshwater, London Bubble, Creative Partnerships, Drama Workhouse, Lambeth Youth Council and others.

How did you get your first job as a freelance drama teacher?

It was an Applied Theatre module at University that gave me my first experience of teaching drama. Then when I left my course, I worked as an administrator, performer and teacher for a small theatre company called Imagination Productions. This gave me a great grounding in all aspects of running a company, which provided me with plenty of experience to then work as a freelancer and set up my own company. As a freelancer, my first work was with children's parties for a company called Splodge. Here I developed my love of interactive story adventures with children. Running a workshop in character with a very clear beginning, middle and end, almost like a bridge between workshop and performance. I do believe the best teachers of theatre practice have plenty of hands on experience in making theatre. My workshop facilitation has always gone hand in hand with my writing, directing and performing.

What advice would you give to someone who wants to be a freelance drama teacher?

Make sure you like children and enjoy the chaos that their energy and passion can bring. I think it's important to have well-planned and structured workshops, but always allow plenty of space for their ideas. Plan workshops carefully for the age you are working with: younger ones may struggle to work in small groups, whereas older ones may need to break out frequently to allow them to create and lead each other.

Start small, volunteer to run some story-times at the library, or a local after-school club. If you're lucky enough to have a theatre or an arts education organisation nearby, offer yourself as an assistant facilitator and learn from your leader. Start to lead warm ups and games.

Make a note of all the games played to increase your repertoire, and always keep a notebook on you to jot down ideas. Take part in other people's workshops as often as possible. Always consider the through-line of your workshop. I learn the thread of my workshop plan in the same way I might learn the lines of a play. Of course, I'm always ready to come 'off script' if the group are veering in a different direction, or if something isn't working. Don't always assume your group will share your vision. A little explanation of why you are playing certain games can go a long way, and help them to learn from the exercises.

What's your favourite drama game?

I love any game that can be adapted to help explore a story. Grandmother's Footsteps is a great one for all ages. For little ones we might be making our way through a dark forest, freezing like trees or creeping up on a sleeping giant. Whereas I might introduce image making, costume and clowning techniques within this game for older ones.

Even when working with teenagers or adults the silly party games can be the best ones to remind them all how to stay playful and engaged. All games should be played for a reason. I keep a record of all my favourite games grouped in a way to help me delve into the relevant list when I need them, whether they are ice-breakers, vocal warm ups or name games, exercises to aid character development, physical storytelling, improvisation, clown, mask or puppetry. Every session needs some form of warm up to help people feel comfortable and get to know each other.

What is your teaching philosophy in a nutshell?

To help people of all ages find stories and tell them in interesting ways. To use story to help build a more creative curriculum, and help us explore who we are as individuals.

You cannot teach a

man anything, you can

only help him find it

within himself.

— *Galileo Galilei*

FIVE

Being a Good
Drama Teacher

Once you have a good reputation as a freelance drama teacher you may well be cherry picking the best jobs and turning away work. It's a wonderful position to be in, but it can take two to three years to get there. It's really important that once you start getting work that you make a good impression.

As a freelancer you can easily be replaced, therefore it's important to keep your client happy. Most clients will contract you on a per-term basis (11-13 weeks).

Here are some tips on keeping your clients happy:

• Always arrive 15 minutes before the start of a class

• Keep your lesson content varied and exciting. Make sure your students love and look forward to your class

• Always stay enthusiastic even if it's a project you're not particularly enthused by. If your client asks you to direct *Oliver* for the 3rd time this year, why, of course you'd love to!

• Always act professionally. Dress smartly, have good manners, and don't say anything inappropriate

• Keep your class safe. No crazy games, and watch out for hazards in the classroom. I had to part ways with one of my freelance teachers because students in her class were getting injured too regularly. The games she played were *insane*: the worst was called 'natural disasters.' She called out 'flood' and the children had to jump onto each other's backs for protection. Ouch! I asked her to stop this game, but she simply replaced it with other crazy ones. It was a shame as she was good fun and the kids loved her. But after a dozen minor injuries occurred in one term, and two children ended up in A&E on separate occasions—well, as lovely as she was, I couldn't renew her contract.

Social media

- Never post photos of your students online

- Never complain about a job, employer, or student online

- Do not make friends with students or parents on social network sites, *especially* students under the age of 18. Connecting with a student under the age of 18 online is against many child protection contracts

- Don't publish inappropriate photos of yourself online. Your students and employers are likely to look you up and you do not want them coming across a photo of you that's inappropriate

- Do not post anything that you wouldn't be happy for a potential employer, current employer, student, or parent to see. Even social media platforms that you think are private may not be as private as you think, or one day may release your private posts publicly.

It is OK to blog or tweet about your work, so long as you never mention particular names and that you keep the writing positive and professional. Your clients are likely to appreciate the publicity, but it's a very good idea to check with them first.

Creating a safe space

My teaching philosophy is, 'create a safe space where students can fully be their creative selves.' When I say safe space, I don't mean a padded room where no one can physically injure themselves. I mean a psychologically safe space where students know they will be accepted for who they are. If students feel safe in your class they will be able to improvise, perform, act and be creative. Students should never be afraid of failing, looking stupid or not being liked. Mistakes should be encouraged—celebrated even! Here are some tips for creating a safe space for your students:

- Lay down the rules. *Kindness* and *good listening* are always my top two

- Give constant positive feedback.
  'That's a great freeze frame of a monkey, Laura.'
  'Oh Callum, how sweet of you to help Tom.'
  'Zara, I really believed in the character you were playing then'

- Give out stickers (if your students are under 11)

- Smile

- Don't get frustrated, grumpy, or angry... or at least don't show it!

- Be patient. If you need to explain your drama activity a few times before the class understands, that's OK: don't be hard on them

- Never force a student to do something they don't want to. If they want to sit and watch for a bit that's no problem

- Never put a student on the spot. Instead, let them volunteer themselves

- Always allow a student to say 'pass' if you're playing one of those games where everyone in the circle has a turn. You'll find about a third of students may pass in the first week, but if you don't force it is likely that by week four every single student will participate voluntarily, even the shyest ones. Let students join in when they're ready. If you make them join in too early, some of the shy ones will never join in, which is so sad. Remember: their pace, not yours

- Treat students with respect and they will treat you with respect. Listen to them, be interested in what they have to say and regularly ask them what they think. This doesn't mean having them interrupt your lesson. Speak to them in breaks and before and after class. If you're speaking to them during your class, do it in a structured way. For example,
  'Put your hand up if you'd like to say something about Darren's performance…'
  'Yes, Lily?'

- Never allow anyone to talk or fidget when someone else is performing. Performances need to be given respect. Once a performance is finished, even if it was very short, always clap the performance, and praise it

- Be firm with anyone disrupting your class, but more on this in chapter six, Classroom Discipline

- Nasty words about anyone must not tolerated. Make this very clear from the start. If anyone says something nasty about someone else, give them a firm telling off during class and ask to see them afterwards. Warn the student that if they say something nasty about someone else a second time they might be asked to leave the group.

Communicating with parents

- Always greet each parent when they drop their child off. A quick smile and hello is enough. Many parents like to know that you're keeping tabs on every grown up entering your classroom, plus it's nice to acknowledge the parent as well as the child

- At the end of the class, try to give a few parents some feedback about how their child did. Try to give positive examples. Try to make sure each parent gets a bit of complimentary feedback about their child at least once a term.

- If a parent is taking too long talking to you (they often do) it's OK to politely excuse yourself and say that you need to speak to another parent. You will always get the teacher-hogging parents! These parents like to talk to you about their child for a very long time. It's not fair to give them all your attention. Make sure to spread your attention evenly between parents

- If a parent wants to watch the class my answer is *always* no. I explain to the parent that having adults watch the class can be off-putting for the other children, and that children settle in much better when their parent isn't watching. It's true.

- Keeping parents happy does not mean giving them everything they want. Remember it's *your* class and you are acting in the best interest of the whole class, not the individual with the pushiest parent. Some parents will try it on and will try to make you give their child special attention or treatment. Don't give these parents want they want, it's not fair on the others.

- The main problem you will have with parents is the week after the casting of your show. You will get parents bribing, begging and guilt-tripping you into re-casting the show and giving their child a bigger part in the show. Never give into this. Once the casting is done, it's done. If a parent is upset about the casting, explain to them that it is an ensemble piece and that there will be lots for their child to do.

Communications with clients

- Do as your client asks. If they want you to direct *Little Shop of Horrors,* and you don't like that musical… too bad. They are paying you, so do as they say during the hours that you work for them. If they start to take advantage, for example they might ask you to do lots of overtime without paying you, then of course you can say no. But if their requests are reasonable then you should be a 'yes' person

- Try not to text clients during their time off, unless it's an emergency. Texting on a Sunday night asking for something won't impress your client. If you can, try and ask them when you see them next. They will have many emails and phone calls from parents to deal with, and they'll appreciate it if you don't add to the load. Unless, of course, it's an emergency

- Offer them a cup of something

- Ask when they like invoices to be in by and meet that deadline

- If you feel they might be unhappy about the work you're doing, ask them if there's anything you can do to improve your classes.

Make yourself interesting

If you know how to turn the charisma on, turn it on while teaching. Entertain. Make jokes, be silly, act out scenes, react to students, be overdramatic, do crazy stuff with your voice to get students attention. The more interesting you make yourself the more focus you will get during your lessons. Be careful not to make the class entirely about you, but a little performing on your part will be appreciated by your students.

Put yourself in your students' shoes

If you're working with ten year olds, try to remember what it was like to be ten. Be sympathetic to students and don't brush off their feelings as 'overdramatic.' Be kind and respectful and they will be kind and respectful to you.

Be yourself

Cheesy advice, I know. But it's true. Children and teen-agers can sniff out a phoney in minutes and they will not connect with you if you are pretending to be something you're not. If you are yourself, your students will be more themselves. Plus if you are yourself, you will be more creative, engaging, and likeable.

Be fair

Only tell a student off if you are 100% sure it was them. If you are unfair students will instantly dislike and disrespect you and you will quickly get behavioural problems in your class. Always be fair, treat students equally, and think the best of them.

Teaching at a weekend theatre school

The best thing about teaching at a weekend theatre school is that you will get the students at the start of the day when they are full of energy. You can make the lesson content of a morning class much more jam-packed and challenging than you could for an after-school club.

Although you want your students to learn, you must remember this is not school. The students will know they don't have to come to your class, and if they stop enjoying it, they will stop coming. Luckily you're teaching a really fun subject, so you should be fine. Just be careful not to strip the fun out of drama. Sometimes during the show term teachers can become over-stressed and take the show too seriously. That's when they may find some of their students dropping out.

Rehearsals need to be fun. It's better to have a slightly unpolished show that students have enjoyed rehearsing, than to produce a polished show but have few students who want to come back next term. Keeping your lessons fun, but professional, is something you should always be striving for. To make lessons fun I recommend that *you* have fun. If you're enjoying the lesson, then so will your students.

Don't be afraid to play drama games you enjoy, or to teach something you are passionate about, or to experiment. Problems come when you are bored of the material you are teaching. The students will pick up on that. Humour, fast-paced lessons, and the odd bit of spontaneity, go down well.

You should always join in with the games and improvisations: the students will love seeing your acting abilities.

Even if you're not a great actor, they love to have you joining in, because if *you're* joining in, it must be good, right?

Teaching an after-school club

You will see students directly after their school day has wrapped up so they might be tried, fed up of sitting down all day, and some of them may be hungry. But don't worry. You will quickly be able to brighten them up. Ask them to sit in a circle and allow them to have a snack and a drink. After 10 minutes, take your register and begin the class. Keep the content of the class interesting and active. I normally start with some very high energy drama games to make the clear distinction between the drama club and school. The last thing they want is more school. However, this doesn't mean you shouldn't be strict. You can be fun and strict at the same time. Think *Mary Poppins*. But more on discipline later.

THE INTERVIEW

Sally Catlin, Principal and Managing Partner of Stagecoach Theatre Arts, Chiswick

What do you like to see in a covering letter?

Something that shows me the applicant has taken the time to find out who the organisation, and I, am – making the letter personal. It's important they sound passionate, and provide an insight into what they can deliver, and how that matches my needs. Applicants should never do a blanket email, or ask the recipient to refer to their Spotlight profile, it is deemed lazy! Stating previous experience of working with children in performing arts settings is preferable. It's essential to attach a CV to the covering letter, and never just send a CV without a cover letter/ email. We get loads of CVs, and timing can be crucial. But persistence on behalf of the applicant goes a long way, and is appreciated.

How can someone impress you in an interview?

I like people to have energy, enthusiasm, good eye contact and passion about working with young people. It's good when people can answer questions precisely, without having to spend too long thinking about the answer. It's also impressive if they show a keen interest in the company, the role and enquire about the students.

What do you think makes a good teacher?

All the above! Plus punctuality, and taking the job seriously, rather than just as a part-time gap-filler. Commitment and consistency are key. Preparation is important, and it's good to get to know the names of students and to be able to identify individual needs. A good teacher should make learning fun and provide a diverse syllabus. They should also have the ability to take constructive criticism, without getting defensive, and be able to work well alongside other teachers. It's essential for the teacher to be able to improvise - they have to be prepared to change tack and go with the flow. Discipline and control are important, a teacher should never resort to shouting, nor should they be 'friends' with students. They have to be in command of their class, while giving students a voice, and a safe place to make mistakes.

What advice would you give to someone who wants to be a freelance drama teacher?

Do your homework and take it seriously. The better prepared and equipped you are, the more likely you'll see results and gain respect from students. It's incredibly rewarding to see students develop, and the difference you can make to them. Be prepared to drop everything at short notice if a call comes looking for cover work, as very often this can be your foot in the door.

I think there's some
connection between
absolute discipline and
absolute freedom.

— *Alan Rickman*

SIX

Classroom Discipline

Classroom management/discipline is where I see a lot of teachers fail. If you are not in control of your class, they cannot learn, they will not enjoy your lesson and you will not enjoy teaching. Some teachers worry that if they are strict the students won't like them.

However, this is not true. Students like it when their teachers are firm, so long as the teacher is kind, fun and fair at the same time.

Can you remember how frustrating it was at school when a teacher couldn't control a class and the lesson descended into chaos?

Well, maybe that was a good thing if it was a boring subject. But if you're a freelance drama teacher then it's most likely your students are attending your class in their time off, so chances are they do want to do drama. Do not be afraid to be strict, or to tell a student off. Just make sure never to lose your temper, and if you do tell someone off, do it in a calm and fair manner. Remember *you* are the teacher, not your students. That's not to say you can't get ideas from students—it's great when they contribute constructively to your lesson—but you must take charge and act like a leader, otherwise you may get eaten alive.

If you do have challenging, or dominating, students in your class, you must be very strict with those particular individuals, otherwise *they* will be running your class and not you. Feel free to put people on time out, or ask them to take a few minutes out of a game or ask them to see you after class. Gulp! Only ever punish the individual who was responsible for the misbehaviour. Never punish the whole class as that's never fair.

Ninety-five per cent of the time it's best to discipline students with positive reinforcement strategies. However, there will be times when you will have to turn on the *scary voice*. By the scary voice, I do *not* mean shouting. I mean a deep firm voice that shows you are displeased by a certain behaviour. Apparently—according to my students—my scary voice was accompanied by 'the eyebrow-raise'! I did joke with them about this during breaks, but it was taken very seriously if ever it was used in practice, which was only about once a term.

The best course I ever went on to improve my teaching skills was Bigfoot's Advanced Behaviour Management course. It will take up only one day of your life, it's very reasonably priced and the chances are it will change your teaching life for the better. You'll be able to step into a classroom stress–free (well, almost) after acquiring the skills they teach you.

Discipline tools for three- to eleven-year-olds

Signal for silence

Shortly after you've taken the register, establish your signal for silence. The best signals for silence are those where the teacher says something and the children re-spond with something else. For example, you say 'Oliver' and put your hands on your head and the class say 'Twist' whilst doing jazz hands. Once you've demonstrated your signal for silence, practise it a few times with the children and then make sure you use it several times during the lesson so they remember it. Create a new signal for each term so it doesn't become stale.

Be firm

Children like boundaries and they will test you to see where yours are. If you've made a rule, stick to it no matter what. You need to keep your rules black and white and do not budge.

Don't give in to a cute smile, a tantrum or blackmail—for example, 'I'm telling my Mum on you!'

Use humour

Act in a slapstick way if you can—they'll love it. A little toilet humour goes down well too (just make sure you keep it appropriate). Never use humour to belittle or make fun of a child. On the other hand, the children will love it if you make fun of yourself.

Smile! And they'll smile back at you

Children have a tendency to mirror your mood. After all, mirroring is how they've learnt to talk, walk and do everything else. If *you* show any signs of a bad mood, so will your class. Be warned.

Regular breaks

Give the children a 5–10 minute break after every 40–50 minutes of teaching. This break is a good time for them to go to the toilet, have a drink and possibly even have a snack. Break time is also a good time for you to bond with the children. Ask them questions and make sure you're interested in what they have to say. They'll love telling you all about themselves and then later on, when you're teaching, they'll be much more likely to listen to what *you* have to say. Encourage the children to use the toilet during the set breaks, not during your class, otherwise it will ruin the flow of your lesson. However, if someone really does look desperate during class, it's a good idea to let him or her go.

One instruction at a time

If they're given too many instructions at a time, children freeze like bunnies staring into headlights or lose focus and misbehave. When explaining a game or activity, take one small step at a time; try not to explain the whole thing at once.

Interesting lesson content

Make sure your lesson content is at the right level for your class. If your lesson content is too hard or too easy, your students will lose focus and may get naughty. Follow your instinct with this; you'll know by their faces whether you've got it right.

Remind them of two golden rules at the start of every lesson

Be kind and *listen* are mine. You may want to think of your own, but make sure your rules are explicit in telling them what to do.

Give examples of what's right and what's wrong

Try to do this in a humorous way. For example, I might say: 'Please can I have you all sitting nice and still when Jasmine performs her poem?' I will then show the children what sitting well looks like: 'Like this,' I'll say, 'and not like this.' Then, I'll slouch, kick my feet about, go in a huff and pretend to pick my nose. They will laugh, and understand how to sit nicely. Giving physical examples of the right and wrong behaviour is a really effective way to communicate with children.

Timeout

Explain clearly at the start of each term, and perhaps a couple of times during the term, the rules of 'timeout'.

These rules are: if you talk when someone's talking or do something not very nice, you'll get a warning. Then, if you do it again, you'll go on a timeout. Make sure everyone knows that a timeout is a big deal. Timeout involves sitting on the naughty chair for two minutes, facing the wall. The parents should also be told if their child has been on a timeout.

Always give one warning before putting someone on a timeout and explain clearly to the child why they have been given that warning; for example, 'Harper, I'm giving you a warning because you were talking to Rosie when Muhammad was performing. One more thing and it will be a timeout.'

If Harper is guilty of a second offence during the lesson, for example, if she pinches Muhammad, she will immediately go on a timeout. Explain to her that you gave her a warning so the punishment is fair. Once Harper has done her two minutes on the chair, be sure to give her a fresh start by saying something like, 'I know you can be good, shall we start again?' If she agrees, shake her hand and say 'good choice'. In the unlikely event that she says 'no', tell her how sad that is and then ask her to go back on the timeout chair.

The chances are that she will agree to be good and join in, or perhaps she does need a few more minutes on the chair. When she agrees to behave well, congratulate her and shake hands on it. Even if she's good for the remainder of the lesson, you will still need to follow through by telling her parents that she went on a timeout. However, when telling her parents about the incident, try to balance it with something positive that she did during the lesson.

Stickers

Get a really beautiful packet of stickers and give them out throughout your lessons. Not too many or they'll lose their value, but not too sparingly or they'll feel unattainable. Always accompany the sticker with a compliment that the whole class can hear: 'Rachel, that was beautiful singing and I noticed that you helped Tom get up on stage. That was kind.' Soon, you will find everyone in the class is trying to help others and sing beautifully. The children need to be constantly reminded of what good behaviour is so they can aspire to it.

Performer of the week

Once a week, give a certificate to someone who did something special during the lesson. If it's a large class, give two out. Make a big deal of the certificate: print it on some coloured card, and tell the children how they could take it home and put it on their fridge or in their bedroom. Keep a note of who gets it each week; try to make sure everyone gets a certificate at least once a term. Find the good in even the most challenging of children—a confidence boost might be just what they need.

Focus on the positive, not the negative

Praise the children and keep your use of the word 'no' to an absolute minimum. If you have a challenging child, praise them the moment they do something good. If your class is struggling to get into a circle, thank the people who are trying.

Discipline for teenagers

Some of these classroom management techniques can also be used with teenagers. The signal for silence, being firm and focusing on the positive rather than the negative all work with older students too. But be careful when working with teenagers not to treat them like children—if you do, they will rebel against it.

The most important thing is to respect them and treat them as equals. Very often the reason teenagers misbehave is because they are bored or feel like they are being treated like children. Don't dumb down lessons for teenagers; teach them the advanced stuff you learned at drama school or university.

This age group, although wonderfully creative and great fun to be around, have a tendency to get wild and show off to each other. You may witness a lot of flirting, showing off and boisterous behaviour. Try to channel this energy into the drama exercises. I recommend treating them with respect, but at the same time do be strict and have a 'zero tolerance for bad behaviour' policy. If someone disrupts your lesson, calmly ask them to leave the class for a few minutes. Then at the end of the lesson ask them to stay behind to talk to you, talk to them about how their behaviour disrupted your class and get to know them a little better, ask them questions, they may want to talk to you about what's bothering them. If they do, listen.

THE INTERVIEW

Holly Dabbs, Freelance Participatory Artist

B.A in Drama, Applied Theatre and Education at Royal
Central School of Speech and Drama.

Which companies do you currently work for?

I work as a freelance Participatory Artist for The Horni-
man Museum, London Transport Museum, The BBC at
The Edinburgh Festival, Nimble Tots in Bath, Preservation
Trust and End of The Road Festival.

Which companies have you worked for previously?

Theatre Bugs, Nimble Arts, Roundhouse, Tea Dance for
Little People, Creative Homes, The Egg Theatre in Bath,
The Rondo Youth Theatre in Bath and the Young Actors
Theatre in London.

How did you get your first job as a freelance drama teacher?

I have always been involved in theatre since joining a
youth theatre when I was 8 years old. After leaving university I worked at the Roundhouse in their Youth team.
I then trained as a primary school teacher and taught
across London for three years. Throughout the school holidays I would work on youth projects. In 2015 I decided
to leave teaching and become a freelance Participatory
Artist.

What advice would you give to someone who wants to be a freelance drama teacher?

Be flexible, adaptable and open to new learning. Be positive with every encounter; remember you are always on show to future employers who could be parents, members of the public or even your participants! However painful, networking is key, building professional relationships and showing interest in the current happenings in the creative world.

What's your favourite drama game?

Zip Zap Boing. I have been playing this game since I was 6 and still play it with all the groups I work with!

What's your teaching philosophy in a nutshell?

I aim to create inclusive work, which fosters a love of creativity and collaboration in all I work with.

Good directors can
bring certain things out of
you, with their intensity or
gentleness or sensitivity
or understanding.
They can make an actor
feel he can do no wrong.

— *Robert De Niro*

SEVEN
Directing a Show

As a freelance drama teacher you will have to direct shows. This was my favourite part of the job, but some drama teachers hate it. I've noticed that the people who don't like directing young casts are usually those who take on scripts that are too long, or over-ambitious. When you direct a show, keep it short and simple so that you and the cast have the space to be creative and enjoy the process. Enjoyment is the main thing to remember when directing a show.

People don't mind if the show isn't perfect; a few mistakes here and there can be cute. But people *will* mind if the cast don't enjoy rehearsing or performing the show.

The worst thing you can do, as a drama teacher, is stress your cast out or overwork them to the point where you put them off drama. The easiest way to avoid this is by making sure that you don't bite off more than you and your cast can chew. Be sure to pack the show with plenty of ensemble numbers, music, and short scenes. Most importantly, stay positive and calm.

Choosing the show

If you're running your own club you will get to choose the show. If you're working for a company, they may ask you which production you'd like to do. Some companies may tell you which show to put on. But if you do get to choose your show, I recommend doing something with plenty of parts, lots of ensemble work and something you know will be popular with your students. Musicals work well as there are often lots of group numbers and there are many great musicals to choose from.

If you are doing a play, I recommend adding lots of music to liven it up. For plays, you can use music to accompany physical theatre, between scenes and even to underscore scenes. My silver package includes a fully licensed musical score for *Alice in Wonderland*. You can also obtain licensed music from production music libraries, for a fee.

You will also need to find a script suitable for your students' age range. Typically one script will work for 3–7-year-olds, another for 7–11-year-olds, and another for 11–21-year-olds. In my silver package there are already-prepared, licence-free versions of *Alice in Wonderland* for each of these age ranges.

Length of the show

I see so many people, especially with 9-11-year-olds, deliver a 90-minute show badly when they could have a delivered a 45-minute show brilliantly. Less-and-polished is much better than more-and-rough when it comes to your show. Here are my show length recommendations:

- 3–7 year-olds: 15 to 20 minutes

- 9–11 year-olds: 40 to 50 minutes

- 12–19 year-olds: one hour to 90 minutes.

Licensing

Many organisations and drama teachers don't get a licence for the play or musical they are going to perform. However, if the work is still in copyright, this can be unlawful and they do so at their own risk.

If you want to buy a licence, here some options:

Josef Weinberger Ltd Musical Theatre

Their shows are costly but very high quality. You can purchase the licence for classics such as *Annie, Fame, Hairspray, High School Musical, Les Miserables* and *The Lion King.*

www.josef-weinberger.com/musicals/ shows-young-performers.html

Theatrical rights

These people own the copyright to *Grease* and some other big-name musicals. You will need to apply directly for a quote.

www.theatricalrights.com/shows

Musicline

They have lots of very affordable lesser-known musicals. Once I had good fun with their musical *Olivia*, a knock-off of *Oliver!*

www.musiclinedirect.com

Treepress

These people have lots of great plays and musicals in-cluding *The Borrowers.*

www.treepress.org

Roald Dahl

If you want to put on a Roald Dahl production you can contact the Roald Dahl organisation to find out about license fees.

www.roalddahl.com/create-and-learn/join-in/perform

Drama Fountain

On my website you can purchase *Alice in Wonderland* as part of the silver package. And in the future I'll be adding more plays, with music included, licensed for performance.

Writing and devising

You could devise a show with students. If you are going to devise a show, make sure to give yourself plenty of time as it can be a lengthy process. I recommend reading up on scriptwriting. I personally love the screenwriting book *Save the Cat* by Blake Snyder. He provides a beat sheet, which I have found to be hugely useful for the devising process.

You could also adapt a show from a book that is out of copyright and in the public domain. Here are some examples of stories out of copyright that you may wish to adapt:

- *Alice's Adventures in Wonderland* by Lewis Carroll

- Anything written by Shakespeare

- Anything written by Charles Dickens, *Oliver Twist* and *A Christmas Carol* being his most popular

- *The Railway Children*, plus anything else by E. Nesbit

- *Grimms' Fairy Tales* by Jacob and Wilhelm Grimm

- *Little Women*, by Louisa May Alcott

- Anything by Jane Austin, *Pride and Prejudice* being her most popular

- *Treasure Island* by Robert Louis Stevenson

- *The Jungle Book* or *Just So Stories* by Rudyard Kipling

- *Heidi* by Johanna Spyri

- *A Little Princess* or *The Secret Garden*, by Frances Hodgson

- *The Wind in the Willows,* by Kenneth Grahame

- *Jane Eyre,* by Charlotte Brontë

- Anything by Oscar Wilde, his most popular being *The Importance of Being Earnest*

- *One Thousand and One Nights* (i.e. Aladdin).

When writing the adaptations, take from these original sources and not some of the many secondary sources that have been written by others and which will very likely still be in copyright.

Auditioning students

It's important you audition students and don't just hand out parts to those students you think will do them well. I give out small audition scripts during the first week and audition students in week two. Dyslexic students and slow readers need a week to practice their audition script. After the auditions work out the cast list at home with a register as a reference, so you know that everyone is included. In week three give out the parts and scripts.

Make sure each student gets at least one line in the show, even if that means you have to scribble extra lines into the script. I firmly believe everyone should get at least one line, even if it's as simple as, 'VILLAGER SIX: Welcome to our village.'

If you audition and cast your show fairly then the whole rehearsal process and show will go much better. There will be a good feeling with the cast and they will respect you and the show more.

Top tips on how to direct a show

- Keep the show simple. Have two or three complex scenes, but keep the majority of the scenes simple. Don't get bogged down with sets, costumes and lights. Less is more

- Rehearse with your props from day one

- Ensemble work works best. Try to get the full cast involved as much as possible

- Be organised. Stick to your timetable. Know what you are rehearsing when. Always take cast lists, blocking plans and extra scripts to your rehearsals

- I recommend breaking rehearsals up with drama games every 20 - 45 minutes. The younger the students, the more breaks you'll need. You will get far more out of the students this way

- Have plenty of full run-throughs: a minimum of four, but preferably six

- Take director's notes. It's OK to stop and start students during your run-throughs. But make sure to have at least two or three other run-throughs where you stay quiet and let the students make mistakes while you take notes. Try to make the notes as specific as possible and make sure every cast member gets at least one positive mention in the director's notes

- Make it fun. Make sure your script is fun to work with and keep the rehearsals fast paced. Try not to spend too long on a particular scene. If students start to lose enthusiasm, inject some energy and inspiration about how the show could be amazing if they keep going

- Always choose process over product. The rehearsal process is far more important than the show itself.

It's much better that the students enjoy rehearsals and learn and produce a less polished show, than they produce an amazing show which they all ended up hating because their director overworked them. The parents—and your client—will not be expecting a West End show, so don't pressure yourself or the students to put one on

- Maintain positive group dynamics. It's vital that the cast get on well. A fair audition process will help. Treating all students equally, no matter their role in the show, will also do a lot to create a thriving team. This means praising chorus members as much as you do people playing leading roles. Also, try and facilitate friendships: if you see a child looking a little lonely, buddy them up with someone

- Do not make changes once it's blocked. Be decisive. Make decisions quickly and don't change your mind. If you keep changing your mind, you run the risk of confusing the cast and wasting valuable rehearsal time.

Rehearsal timetable

You will need a rehearsal timetable and you will need to stick to it. If you don't, some students may get more time on their scenes than others, which isn't fair, and could result in needing to call extra, emergency rehearsals at the end of term. Calling extra rehearsals will not please the parents, or your client, and it may not even be possible.

You need to stay organised and stick to the timetable.

Here's an example of one of mine.

> *Week one:* Drama games. Announce the show and explain the story and all the parts. Explain to the students that next week you will be running auditions for people who want big parts. Give out audition scripts for the students to go home with and work on. The audition scripts should be tiny, just three or four lines from the original script.
>
> *Week two:* Drama games and auditions.
>
> *Week three:* Give parts and scripts out. Make sure every student has been given a part and at least one line. Do the first read through and explain your vision for the show to the students. Get them excited about the project. If there's time, block scene one.
>
> *Weeks four to seven:* Block the show. (Plan which scenes you will be blocking when.)
>
> *Week eight:* Drama games. One staggered run-through.
>
> *Week nine:* Drama games. Run-through with no stops and take detailed director's notes. Remember to give plenty of praise, even if you think the show is a disaster!
>
> *Week ten:* Two dress rehearsals. You will have asked parents to bring in costumes previously.
>
> *Week eleven:* Run through the show twice. Then show the parents.

As you can see you only get four weeks to block the show. It's not a lot. Divide the scenes up and list which ones you will be doing each week. My Alice in Wonderland script for 7-11 year olds has thirteen scenes, so for this you'd need to do three to four scenes a week.

THE INTERVIEW

Brian Conroy, Owner and Principal of West Oxfordshire Academy of Performing Arts
www.woapa.co.uk

What do you like to see in a covering letter?

A brief description of relevant experience of working with children. Also it's useful when people include their location. Sometimes people apply and they live over 50 miles away, which is not feasible.

How can someone impress you in an interview?

I like interviewees to be organised, on time, presentable, personable and not to 'act!' It's best just to be natural. Some ideas of what they would like to teach/direct is useful. It's good when people ask about the 'style' of the organisation, for example, 'Is it more dance-based?' 'Is it script-based drama?' 'Do you do performances?'

What do you think makes a good teacher?

Good planning—responsive to what may arise and a 'can-do' attitude. It's not good when teachers arrive with just minutes to spare, and then head out the door one minute after the class.

What advice would you give to someone who wants to be a freelance drama teacher?

Don't 'specialise' too much. Singing teachers can also use some 'acting' in their classes—as can dance tutors. It's not useful to say 'I only do this.'

Serious art is born

from serious play.

— *Julia Cameron*

EIGHT

Setting Up an After-School Club

You may have decided you only want to work for already-existing drama groups, in which case skip this chapter. However, I can tell you from first-hand experience that setting up your own after-school club is far more profitable and is not very much work. Many schools are looking for after-school clubs, particularly drama ones, and there are not enough people out there running them. In this chapter I will show you how to set up your own.

When I lived in the Bath area I was running five after-school clubs a week and earning far more than I ever
thought possible as a freelance drama teacher.

The benefits of setting up your own after-school club

The pay

By setting up your own after-school club, you can earn
£30 to £90 per hour. You will be charging each student
£3 per class. Yes, cheaper than childcare. At £3 a class if
you get twenty children signed up, you make £60. Thirty
in your class and you make £90. But don't be tempted
to charge more per student. I've known people to charge
£5 or £6 for the club and their model failed: they just
didn't get enough students.

The hours

It's short working hours, which you can fit around other
jobs or auditions. You can offer a 1 hour, 1 hour 15 minute, or 1 hour 30 minute club. The club takes place after
the school day finishes; this is slightly different for every
school, but always between 3pm-4pm. Generally, it's at
about 3.15pm.

Creative freedom

If you run your own after-school club, you are the boss.
You choose what you want to teach.

Time off

You will get the school holidays off and if you need more you can take it, providing you can find a cover teacher.

Profit

Setting up your own club is more profitable than working for a pre-existing group. If you work for a company, they tend to take a large cut of the money being made. If you run the after-school club yourself, you take 100% of the money.

It's fun

The children come to have fun—and so should you.

It's equal opportunity

If you're a drama teacher for a theatre school or theatre company, you will inevitably get a certain type of student: children with parents who are willing to give up their Saturday morning to drive their child to class. But what about all the other young people with parents not willing to take them? Often, these children don't get to do dance or drama unless there is a reasonably priced after-school club available at their school. And if they still can't afford your club, you could consider giving out a few free places. I gave out two free places a term in each of my after-school clubs. I asked the headteacher of the school if there were any students who like drama but whose parents wouldn't be able to afford the club. If the head teacher said yes (they always did), I gave these students a free place in the club.

What to do, step-by-step

- Get **public liability insurance.** You'll pay a yearly fee for the certificate and it will cover all your classes. It should cost £100-200 a year. Phone around insurance companies and get several quotes

- Take a **first aid course.** The Red Cross and St John Ambulance both offer good courses across the UK

- Get a **criminal records check** through the government's DBS agency. If you don't already have one, you may need to volunteer or work as a teaching assistant to get one. You can't apply for one directly yourself

- **Contact the right schools.** To make this model work, do not contact schools with fewer than 200 students. These schools are too small and you will not get enough students in your club to make it financially viable. You can expect to get about 10% to 15% of students trying your drama group out. So for a school of 200 you'll get around 20 students signing up, for a school of 300 students you'll get around 30 in your class. If the school has 500 or more students, consider offering them two clubs, for example, one on a Wednesday and one on a Thursday. To find local schools you can put your postcode into this website:

www.schoolsnet.com. It will show you all the schools in your area and give you the number of students

- Write to all the **schools with over 200 students** within travelling distance and ask if they would like an after-school club. Tell them who you are, that you have insurance and a DBS check, what your club will do, your available days and how much you will charge per student. Write to every school you are willing to travel to. The more schools you write to the better. Getting the first club can be hard, which is why you should write to dozens of schools. But once you get one school, getting more on board will much easier. Once you have your first after-school club, write *again* to all the same schools, telling them about the success of your drama club at the first school and ask them for second time if they would like a drama club. The chances are you will get a lot more takers the second time around

- **Price it right.** Charge £3 per student for your after-school club (£33 for an 11 week term). At £3 each, you do not need to offer sibling discounts. Charge per term, not per week, otherwise your class numbers will fluctuate, and it will turn into admin hell. Parents need to pay for the whole term, even if they are going on holiday and will miss two weeks

- If a school is interested, they will invite you to a **meeting**. 80% of the time the school won't charge you for the use of their school hall. If they do, normally it's such a low fee that it's worth your while accepting their rate. The most I ever paid for a school hall was £8 for the hour

- Once you've agreed the arrangements with the school, you can **send letters out to parents** inviting students to your club. You can give these letters to the school reception and they will distribute them to the correct year groups. On this letter you should include a free trial booking form. It's important on this booking form to ask for parental contact details and whether the student has any medical conditions or allergies that you need to be aware of

- I offered my after-school clubs to years 3, 4, 5 and 6 (7–11 year olds), but you may want to offer your services to other age groups

- For the first club of each term, you should **offer a free trial** with no obligation for students to join afterwards

- You should never take more than 30 students in a class. Talk to your public liability insurance company and check with them how many children you are covered for in one class. Normally it's up to 30

- Before your first class you need to do a **health and safety risk assessment** of the space you'll be using. You can download a form from the government's website at *www.hse.gov.uk*, or the school may have one you can use. Ask the school to allocate you a time to assess the space. Then do so. File the completed risk assessment away carefully

- **Bring a register** to your first class. Make sure that you have every child's name written down somewhere, as well as details of any medical conditions you need to be aware of and their parents' contact numbers

- Take a register and **do a head count** to be doubly certain

- Make sure your free trial is **awesome**!

- After your free trial class, **give out a letter** to students that they must give to their parents. In this letter explain how parents can pay fees for the term. I always say cash or a cheque and they can hand it in to me or to the school reception.

THE INTERVIEW

Rhiannon Wallace, Actress and freelance drama teacher

Which companies do you currently work for as a freelance drama teacher?

Jigsaw Arts.

Which companies have you worked for in the past?

Pauline Quirke Academy.

Did you go to university or drama school and if so which one and what did you study?

I studied at the Royal Central School of Speech and Drama; my degree was in Acting specializing in Collaborative and Devised Theatre.

How did you get your first job as a freelance drama teacher?

A friend of mine was a principal at an academy and they had a vacancy for a teacher to teach their 3-4 and 5-6 year old classes. I was initially daunted by the prospect because I hadn't had much experience, only as a teaching assistant in mainstream and SEN (special educational needs) schools.

What advice would you give to someone who wants to be a freelance drama teacher?

Take all the advice you can get, especially at the beginning. Every class is different, every child is different, and every week has a new challenge. It's helped me grow in confidence and it's forced me to be organised; I love it. As an actor it keeps me on my toes. I'm learning and teaching new games, vocal warm ups, songs and even basic dance routines.

What's your favourite drama game?

That's a tough one; there are so many great games! My favourite focus game with the younger age groups is The Key Game. It's a circle game and it requires a lot of concentration and it is an especially good game to play if the group has a lot of energy and you need to calm them down after a dance routine. Everyone stands in a circle and one person stands in the middle of the circle with their eyes shut. This is very important and it's so interesting which students can trust the rules of the game and keep their eyes shut and those that cheat! Everyone in the circle passes around the 'noisy' keys until I call stop. At that moment everyone puts their hands behind their backs and the person in the middle opens their eyes. The person in the middle now has to guess who's got the keys. It's a really exciting moment! Some students cannot contain themselves and will ultimately give the game away by pointing at their friend who is hiding the keys. Some students have excellent poker faces and are never caught, others get the giggle fits. It's brilliant!

What's your teaching philosophy in a nutshell?

Have fun. There is no point in teaching drama or making theatre with young people unless they have fun. I think this works across all age groups. You can have expectations, but if your expectations override the fun, then what's the point? At the end of the day they're paying me, not the other way around. So if I don't make it fun and interesting they'll find another drama teacher.

NINE

Insurance, Health and Safety

Public Liability Insurance

If you are running your own after-school club you will need your own public liability insurance.

However, even if you are working for other companies, they will often ask you to get your own public liability insurance too.

The insurance should cost you £100-300 pounds a year, depending which company you go with and how many students you are teaching. Phone around and get a few quotes.

I used Protectivity; they were always clear, helpful and well priced. *www.protectivity.com*

It's crucial to keep your insurers updated with how many classes you are teaching and how many students are in each class to ensure that your cover remains valid.

If you are a member of Equity you may be covered for public liability insurance already. Contact them to find out.

DBS check

You will need a government Disclosure and Barring Service Check (DBS) to work with children. It is not possible for an individual to get a DBS check done on themselves. To get one you will need a company or school to do it for you. If you are starting out as freelance drama teacher you may find it difficult to get your first job without a DBS check. Getting a DBS check done is another advantage of volunteering or working as a teaching assistant.

Child protection

If you are working for a client it is very likely they will provide you with a copy of their child protection policy.

Here's an example policy.

Question any unknown adult who enters the premises.

Never allow pupils access to your personal social networking sites.

All students are to be treated equally with respect and dignity.

Always check a space is safe before allowing students in. Make sure the fire exits are clear and that there are no sharp or dangerous objects in the room.

Know what to do in case of a fire.

Conduct yourself in a good manner with pupils. No drinking, swearing or smoking.

Keep student information confidential.

Never use physical force against a student, unless it constitutes reasonable restraint to protect him/her or another person.

Never engage in rough, physical or sexual games.

Never use—or tolerate pupils' use of—inappropriate language.

Always work in an open environment. Never allow yourself to be left alone with one pupil. If you need to take a child to the toilet, take two children or more, so that you are not left alone with one child. If one child is left behind at the end of the class, go and stand with someone else too, perhaps a school receptionist, or another member of staff. Be certain not to be left alone in a room with one child.

If you notice any child with injuries or behaviours that are suspicious, report it to the director of the company or headmaster or headmistress of the school.

Sometimes touch is necessary when teaching drama. But it should never be used as a form of punishment, it should only be used to demonstrate particular drama activities. It is important for staff to be sensitive to a pupil's reaction to physical contact and to act appropriately. No pupil should ever be touched on a part of his/her body or in a way that is indecent, or could be thought to be.

If a student tells you something serious, perhaps that they are being abused by someone, or that they are self-harming, then you must tell someone within the organisation you are working for, either a headmaster or headmistress or specialist child protection officer. If a student asks you to keep a secret, you must explain to them that you may need to tell another trustworthy adult.

Handing students over to parents

When your class has finished it's your responsibility to get all the students back with their parents safely. Many teachers let the parents pile into their classroom and take the children. This is not a safe way to have your students collected. It's your responsibility to make sure that every child goes home with the right adult, and that no one gets lost or abducted once your class has finished.

With children under the age of eleven, I always ask them to sit in a circle in the classroom. I ask the adults to queue up and wait outside the classroom, then, one by one, I let each child go once I have seen their parent or guardian.

Preventing accidents

Even if you are working for a company, if an accident happens during your class you could be the one who is liable if you are found to have been negligent.

- Always make sure stacked chairs are secure and not stacked too high

- Keep children off stacked chairs

- Keep fire exits clear

- Keep your classroom door shut and don't let any strangers in

- Keep your games safe

- No socks on slippery surfaces

- Clear up any food or drink spillages that may be hazards

- Keep coats and bags off the floor

- Keep your space clear of tripping hazards

- Make sure you have control over your class and a signal for silence

- Know the fire procedure

- Always keep a mental and written note of how many students are in your class. Do regular head counts

- If you're moving to a different room during the class, do a head count when you leave a room and another when you enter a new room

- Don't let any children out of your sight

- No games that involve students jumping on each other's backs or legs.

Invoicing

As a freelance drama teacher, you'll be expected to invoice the client for the work you've done.

Always include:

- Your name, address and contact details

- The date of the invoice

- Your bank details

- The details and dates of the work

- The invoice total

- An invoice number. Starting from 1 and counting

upwards is fine, but don't use the same invoice number twice even if you have several clients.

Keep all your invoices together and in a safe place, as you'll need them for your tax return.

Tax

If you haven't already done so you need to register with HMRC as self-employed. You'll need to register for Self Assessment tax returns and Class 2 National Insurance at the same time. You'll then be able to report your self-employment income through regular tax returns.

You can do it here: *www.gov.uk/set-up-sole-trader/register*

Be sure to keep track of all your drama teaching income and outgoings throughout the year. Keep receipts for things you buy to use in your class, such as props, stickers, stationery, and so on. You can claim these things back on your tax return as business expenses. But I am afraid you usually cannot claim for other costs such as travel, clothes, and food.

Completing your tax return is not as hard as it sounds especially if you do it online. But if you don't want to do your own tax return you can get an accountant to do it for you. They will probably charge £200-300 to do the return. Their quote will depend on your earnings.

Once you're earning a full-time income, an accountant may save you more money than the cost of their fees because they know exactly what you can claim legally in business expenses.

A compromise solution is to use a software package designed to help you with your returns. HMRC provides a list of accredited packages here: *www.gov.uk/software-tax-returns*

Do make sure to put away enough tax money each month so that you don't have a shock at the end of the year. You can calculate how much tax you will need to put away here:
www.gov.uk/guidance/hmrc-tools-and-calculators

You will normally be a sole trader, which is the simplest form of self-employment. But some drama companies use other structures, including partnerships. Make sure you understand exactly what your relationship with your client is, because it will affect how you complete your tax returns.

THE INTERVIEW

Lauren Senatore, Managing Director at Bigfoot Arts Education

What do you like to see in a covering letter?

First and foremost I like to see passion! I need to know that this person firmly believes in the use of the arts as an educational tool and that they share Bigfoot's ethos regarding creative learning. I also like to see a very brief summary of their relevant work experience and some carefully chosen career highlights. They will also need to mention why they wish to work for my company and it's important that I come away with the impression that this is because they believe in what we do and not just because they need a job!

How can someone impress you during an interview?

The answer to this is absolutely research, research, research! The times where I have been most impressed by interviewees is when they have been able to show me that they already have an in-depth knowledge of Bigfoot, before they have even been offered a job! Being able to reference facts about Bigfoot and how we work, or perhaps the education/career of members of the Bigfoot team, makes it obvious that they have taken the time to thoroughly read the whole of the website or to even have researched our LinkedIn profiles. This demonstrates to me firstly that they are taking the position seriously, and secondly, that they are genuinely interested in us and what we do.

What do you think makes a good teacher?

Somebody with a strong rapport with children and young people, someone who can walk the line between having fun and maintaining good behaviour and is able to pitch their teaching style accordingly, someone who loves what they do, and finally, someone with a strong sense of commitment. Commitment is important for teaching for all sorts of reasons: committing to putting in the time to thoroughly prepare their lessons, committing to a regular booking so that the children receive that all-important consistency, and committing to the fact that, a lot of the time, your work with the children will not end once your lesson ends. There is so much more to working with children than what takes place in the classroom.

What advice would you give to someone who wants to be a freelance drama teacher?

Gain as much experience as you can (this may involve volunteering), learn from others who have been doing the job for longer than you, attend as much CPD (continuing professional development) as you possibly can and when working – always ask for and learn from feedback.

Contacts

Short Courses for Drama Teachers

There are many outstanding short courses. Here are my recommendations; I asked each provider to explain what they offer.

Bigfoot Arts Education

Bigfoot runs an extensive training programme for arts facilitators as well as classroom teachers. Over the past 16 years Bigfoot has built up a reputation for being at the forefront of training for drama workshop leaders as well as creative CPD for teachers. Whether you are just starting to think about drama workshop leading as a supplement to your acting career, or whether you are already an established facilitator, our training courses will offer high quality, skills-based learning and a chance to network with likeminded people. The courses provided are:

- Advanced Behaviour Management

- Multi-Sensory Workshops with Early Years and KS1

- How to Create Devised Theatre With Children

- Crash Course In Drama Workshop Leading

- Drama Games and Exercise Masterclass

Check out the training page on the website for more details: *www.bigfootartseducation.co.uk*

Drama Resource

Drama Resource offers a range of high quality training courses for teachers and freelance practitioners in London, Manchester and elsewhere. Our drama in education courses explore the role of drama across the curriculum, as well as using drama to raise standards in English. Theatre professionals run masterclasses on directing and devising theatre, improvisation and mask, to help improve group performances.

All our courses are highly practical and supported by explanatory notes, enabling participants to easily adapt approaches for their own use. The company also offers in-house training to schools and other organisations.

dramaresource.com/courses

Frantic Assembly

Frantic Assembly runs an extensive training programme for professionals, graduates and young artists. The programme provides specialist skills training for individuals pursuing careers in theatre. Activities include regular public workshops, advanced training for professional artists and training for teachers. You can find details of our courses here:

www.franticassembly.co.uk/train/teacher-training/

Email   workshops@franticassembly.co.uk
Phone   020 7841 3115

The National Theatre - Central London

Teachers looking to nurture their passion for theatre and hone their skills can join us at the NT for one of our inspiring professional development opportunities for teachers: Teacher Preview Evenings, CPD Short Courses and annual NT Drama Teacher Conference. CPD Short Courses explore everything from technical theatre skills to the work of key practitioners, playwriting and exploring texts.

Our Drama Teacher Conference runs in February half term each year and is an opportunity for teachers to take part in two days of inspiring professional development with a variety of incredible theatre-makers, including NT artists and staff.

For more information contact learning@nationaltheatre.org.uk.

nationaltheatre.org.uk

Stagecoach Teacher Training

The Associate Diploma in teaching the Performing Arts (ADPA) in Walton, Surrey, is an internationally recognised qualification, listed by Ofqual at Level 4 and awarded by Performance Arts Awards. The two-week course is developed and run by Stagecoach Theatre Arts Ltd and is led by tutors who will support you every step of the way. It is both stretching and stimulating.

We can promise you inspirational teachers, a safe and inclusive environment, exciting, relevant workshops, one-to-one tutoring and a great deal of fun. We also offer a two-day fast track course to cater for experienced teacher who are just looking to gain a qualification.

Some of the topics covered throughout the course:

- Classroom management

- Teaching creatively

- The nuts and bolts of good teaching

- Preparation and planning of lessons

- How to support and enable SEND children

- Child development

- Diversity and inclusivity awareness

- Current child protection issues

- Health and safety issues.

For more information, please visit our website: *www.stagecoach.co.uk/teacher-training* or contact the Stagecoach Education Department:

Email   education@stagecoach.co.uk

Phone   01932 254333

Trestle Theatre Co Ltd

At Trestle, we offer a range of opportunities for freelance drama teachers:

- A group of teachers can get together to book us for Outreach Teacher Workshops. These workshops can take place nationally and internationally. If the teachers do not have space then they can come to the Trestle Arts Base for the workshop.

- Teacher INSET days are for teachers and practitioners alike to attend 1-3 days training in mask, physical theatre and half mask. Sessions are centred around learning new skills and exercises, as well as developing wider understandings of the appropriate pedagogies. More information can be found at: *www.trestle.org.uk/participate/workshops/inset-teacher-and-practitioner-training-2/*

- Trestle has teamed up with Middlesex University to deliver a unique MA course in Education (Drama). The three-year part-time Master's programme is designed for teachers and lecturers of drama, theatre studies and performing arts and will be run at Trestle Arts Base, a contemporary performing arts centre in St Albans, Hertfordshire and home to Trestle Theatre Company. More information can be found at: *www.trestle.org.uk/participate/training/ma-education-drama/*

Potential clients to contact

Here I have listed some of the larger part-time theatre schools and creative companies that have several or sometimes hundreds of schools, spread across the UK. There are many schools I haven't listed in this directory so please do your own personal research for theatre schools and youth theatres in your area. Each company has provided their own listing.

Bigfoot Arts Education

Bigfoot is a national arts education company that sets out to raise standards in education through a creative approach to learning. Bigfoot contracts drama, dance, music and art facilitators up and down the country on a flexible freelance basis. Bigfoot invests in the development of their facilitators by offering a full induction course, a free CPD programme and masterclasses delivered by the likes of Frantic Assembly and Little Angel Theatre, all designed to keep facilitators highly skilled on current techniques and policies. Bigfoot are always on the look-out for new talent and run recruitment sessions once per year. If you are an experienced facilitator with an excellent rapport with children and strong behavior-management skills then Bigfoot would love to hear from you! For further details or to download Bigfoot's application forms please visit: *bigfootartseducation.co.uk/work-for-us/application-form/*

London	Bristol
Sussex	Wales
Kent	The North East
Hampshire	The North West
The South West	The Midlands

Debutots

Debutots run drama classes all over the UK. We are always on the lookout for enthusiastic drama practitioners. Successful applicants receive full training and we provide complete class plans and excellent rates of pay. We are looking for energetic, reliable and imaginative individuals with a genuine desire to work with the early years age group. Your own transport, an enhanced DBS check and previous experience with this age group are beneficial. We are looking for practitioners who can commit for a minimum of 6 months. Resting actors who cannot commit need not apply. Please send your CV to enquiries@debutots.co.uk.

North Down & Ards

Dundonald

East Belfast

South Belfast

Lisburn and surroundings

Durham

Chester-Le-Street

Consett

Hexham

Darlington

Stockton-on-Tees & surroundings

Hull

Beverley

Driffield and Market Weigh-ton

Worcestershire

Wolverhampton

Dudley and surrounding areas

Nuneaton

Dorset

Swindon and surroundings

Gloucester

Cheltenham

Tewkesbury

The Forest of Dean and surrounding areas

Newbury

Thatcham

East and North Hertfordshire

Sutton

Epsom

Wimbledon

Tadworth

Reading and surrounding areas

Brighton

Hove and surrounding areas

Bexley

Bromley and surrounding areas

Chelmsford

Billericay

Brentwood and surrounding areas

Finchley

Hampstead

Muswell Hill

Dramacademy

We provide after-school clubs in many schools in London and Surrey. Our teachers have been teaching children alongside their performance careers for many years and have developed a style of drama workshop that is high-energy fun for children while at the same time helping them to be strong communicators, concentrate and focus for longer periods, improve physicality and to be confident, self-assured individuals.

Email   info@dramacademy.co.uk

www.dramacademy.co.uk/after-school-clubs/

The Helen O'Grady Drama Academy

The Helen O'Grady Drama Academy recruits teachers who have had experience working with children over a period of time. As we are primarily a self-development, not performance-orientated organisation, we seek teachers who are creative and energetic, willing to accept training in our methodology and are committed. All teachers are provided with curriculum material covering each lesson during the academic term and covering age groups from three year olds to adults. Initial and regular ongoing training is provided and all teachers are invited to attend seminars at the beginning of each term to workshop the curriculum for the following term.

Further information can be found on *www.helenogrady.org.uk* and interested teachers wishing to get involved with our academy can contact Nigel Le Page, National Director, at headoffice@helenogrady.co.uk.

Barnet	East Cheshire
Bolton	Edinburgh
Bristol	Enfield
Bromley & District	Exeter
Cambridgeshire	Gloucestershire
Cardiff	Guildford
Croydon	Hertfordshire
Derbyshire	Liverpool
Dorset	Lothian & Borders
Dundee	Merseyside

Monmouthshire

Northampton

North Coventry

North Cumbria

North Leicestershire

North London

North West Ireland

North West London

Nottingham

Oldham

Portsmouth

Preston

Renfrewshire

Sefton

Sheffield

South Downs

South East London

South London

South Manchester

South & Mid Cheshire

South West London

Staffordshire

St Helens

Stockport

Swansea

Tayforth

West Dorset

West London

Wirral

York

Jigsaw Performing Arts

Jigsaw Performing Arts School runs classes in Drama, Dance and Singing for children from 3-18 years at our weekend schools across London, Hertfordshire and Kent. We look for teachers who work in the arts and are passionate about their discipline. We recruit teachers who show us confidence, knowledge of their discipline, warmth and energy. We are always regularly recruiting as many of our teachers do get contracted for plays or films. To find out more or send a CV, contact polly@jigsaw-arts.co.uk.

jigsaw-arts.co.uk

Balham	Harrow
Bexleyheath	Hendon
Brentwood	Ilford
Broxbourne	Mitcham
Camden	Sevenoaks
Crouch End	St Albans
Croydon	Stevenage
Deptford Bridge	Ware
Dulwich	Watford
Ealing	Wimbledon
Enfield	Winchmore Hill
Finchley	

Little Tanks

Little Tanks is always on the lookout for experienced Drama Tutors to run courses at schools situated in Berkshire, Surrey and East Sheen London. The requirement is to run the sessions using your own expertise and experience to ensure the children are having fun and building confidence as well as working towards a small scale presentation to show the parents at the end of the term. Equity status or public liability insurance and a current DBS check are required as well as your base location being within a 40 minute car journey of the venues. Please contact Debi Rush on: tank.deb@talk21.com for a more detailed job description and check out our website: *www.littletanks.co.uk*

Sheen, London	Old Windsor
Mortlake, London	Langley
Weybridge	Slough
Egham	Ascot
Maidenhead	Danesfield
Windsor	Ickenham

Little Voices

Little Voices provides outstanding drama and singing tuition to children across the UK. Our unique framework of lessons means that children are taught in small groups of no more than eight children. We pride ourselves on traditional and inspirational yet fun filled lessons which are taught by passionate and highly qualified tutors whose goal is to ensure that each child excels in a happy environment. We work towards the highly respected and accredited LAMDA examinations in Musical Theatre, Drama, Acting, and Communication Exams. Please send CVs to info@littlevoices.org.uk.

Blackburn	Northwich
Bolton	Peterborough – Stamford
Bridgend – Wales	Peterborough – Stanground
Chester	Peterborough – Werrington
Chester- copy	Preston – Buckshaw Village
Clitheroe	Preston – Chorley
Feniscowles	Preston – Fulwood
Guildford	Preston – Hutton
Kings Langley	Preston – Leyland
London – Fulham	Shelf – West Yorkshire
London – Putney	Stockport
London – Richmond	Tottington
London – Wandsworth	Welwyn Garden City
Lytham St Annes	West Kent
Newcastle – Fenham	Whitchurch
Newcastle – Gosforth	Wigan

Montage Theatre Arts

Montage Theatre Arts is a charity in South East London which provides quality theatrical arts training to students aged 3 to 93 from varying social and economic circumstances. MTA teachers are from a wide range of creative backgrounds but we do ask for long-term commitment, so they are not usually working performers themselves.

To apply, CVs should be sent to office@montagetheatre.com.

One Day Creative Education

One Day is a nationally recognised fresh and for-ward-thinking creative education company, connecting children and learning with creativity and imagination. Our innovative approach to education is the perfect companion for schools looking to enrich the curriculum and complement classroom teaching.

In our experience, children have very different and unique ways of learning and we believe that these individual learning styles should be nurtured and encouraged. Placing children in an environment where they can thrive and feel confident, often leads to successful and happy learning. Our menu of workshops cater for creative learning throughout all Key Stages using drama, music, dance, performance, creative arts and play.

Our professional and experienced facilitators deliver our broad range of participatory workshops with children right across the UK.

We are always on the lookout for passionate, creative practitioners from diverse backgrounds to join our team. For more information, please see our website *www.onedaycreative.com* and enquire about our monthly auditions. Please send your enquiry, CV and covering letter to Artistic Director Stephanie Noble steph@onedaycreative.com.

The Pauline Quirke Academy of Performing Arts

The Pauline Quirke Academy of Performing Arts delivers lessons in Musical Theatre, Comedy & Drama and Film & Television to students aged 4-18. PQA has over 100 Academies UK wide. You can upload your CV on our website *www.pqacademy.com* to be considered for a teaching position. PQA are looking for brilliant, inspirational and energetic teachers who will instil their passion for performing arts into the hearts and minds of the young people who attend their academies. Applicants should be over 21 with professional training or equivalent experience.

Amersham	Cardiff
Aylesbury	Chelmsford
Barnet	Cheltenham
Barnsley	Chislehurst and Sidcup
Bath	Colchester
Beverley	Coventry
Bishop's Stortford	Crawley
Blackpool	Darlington
Bradley Stoke	Dartford
Brentwood	Derby
Bridgnorth	Dulwich
Brighton	Durham
Brighton West	Eastbourne
Bristol	Eastleigh
Cambridge	Edgbaston
Canterbury	Edinburgh

Enfield	Rugby
Evesham	Scarborough
Exeter	Sheffield
Guildford	Solihull
Harlow	Southend on Sea
Harrogate	Southport
Hemel Hempstead	Stratford-Upon-Avon
Hertford	Stroud
High Wycombe	Sutton
Ipswich	Coldfield
Leeds	Swindon
Leicester	Tees Valley
Lichfield	Tonbridge
Maidenhead	Torbay
Milton Keynes	Tunbridge Wells
Muswell Hill	Warwick
Newcastle	Watford
Northampton	Wickford
Nottingham	Windsor
Nuneaton and Hinckley	Wirral
Oxford	Wolverhampton
Plymouth	Woodford Green
Preston	Worcester
Richmond	York
Romford	

Perform

At Perform, we only hire the best people and give them the training they need to do a great job. We train all our teachers before they begin working for us and we continue to offer training to constantly develop their skills. Perform teachers are working actors, singers and dancers with a professional qualification (drama school/university degree) in the performing arts. They must be all-rounders and able to act, sing and dance brilliantly. Most of our staff attend regular auditions and go off to do acting jobs from time to time. However our teachers never think of their work as 'a bit of teaching to pay the bills'. If you have a 3 year qualification in drama, dance or singing, you'll need to attend one of our monthly group auditions. To arrange this, please email your CV, headshot and covering letter to recruitment@perform.org.uk.

Perform have hundreds of schools spread across London and the south of the UK.

Pyjama Drama

Pyjama Drama offers drama and imaginative play classes for children up to 7 years. We look for teachers who have a genuine love of working with young children and the skills to ignite young imaginations through drama, movement, music and play. To find out more visit *pyjamadrama.com* or email sarah@pyjamadrama.com.

Llantrisant, Bridgend & The Vale

Mid & South Powys

North Powys and Wrexham

Pembrokeshire

Bournemouth

Colchester East

Exeter

London (SW)

New Forest

North Surrey

Southampton East

Three Counties

Tunbridge Wells

Aberdeen

South Aberdeenshire & Angus

Calderdale

Dewsbury, Batley & Brighouse

Huddersfield & Mirfield

Leeds North

Mid Cheshire

Newcastle Central

North Cumbria & Tyne Valley

Selby and surroundings

Sheffield (South)

South & West Cumbria

Stockport & Cheshire East

Trafford and Didsbury

Bromsgrove & Redditch

Cheltenham

Tewkesbury

Cotswolds

Gloucester

Stroud

Forest of Dean

Newark

Oswestry & Shrewsbury

Oxfordshire

South Staffs

Telford & Bridgnorth

West Wiltshire

RoughMagicke Drama

RoughMagicke Drama is on the lookout for inspiring drama teachers. Based in Harrow, RoughMagicke has been working with local students for the last 5 years, building confidence in public performance and fostering a love of literature and the broader arts. Past experience of teaching drama and LAMDA is preferred, however, we will support you with in-house training and development. More important is a passion for providing outstanding teaching, dedication to your role and a track record of embracing responsibility. If you seek the flexibility of choosing your own working hours together with the ease of teaching from home or in local schools, then do get in touch today and share your CV with an accompanying cover letter to jo@roughmagickedrama.com. An up-to-date DBS will be required.

www.rmdrama.com

Harrow   Barnet

Watford   Mill Hill

StageAbility

StageAbility offers after-school drama classes for children aged 4-17. Classes suit the budding superstar as well as those who need to build confidence and increase their self-esteem. High energy classes mean that students never get bored, can't wait to get to class and develop a cross section of life skills such as teamwork, confidence, clarity and self-discipline, through a mixture of drama, song and movement. For our regular drama classes, we look for teachers who relish the development of their students and thrive on seeing their growth in confidence. For our theatre shows, we look for teachers who can choreograph and direct children. We are also keen to hear from teachers with specialisms as we run development courses to focus on areas such as comedy, mime, stage fighting, improvisation, and so on. Please contact jackie@berkshire.stageability.co.uk.

Tilehurst, Reading	Burghfield Common, Reading
Earley, Reading	Wokingham

Stagecoach Theatre Arts

Have you got what it takes to teach for the largest UK network of performing arts schools? If so, we would love to hear from you. We are always on the lookout for passionate, inspirational and dedicated teachers. To apply please visit *www.stagecoach.co.uk/work-with-us* and upload your CV.

Stagecoach have hundreds of schools all over the UK. If you go onto the website *www.stagecoach.co.uk* and type in your town, you will probably find their are several, or maybe even many, Stagecoach schools near you.

Steppin Out Stars of Tomorrow

We look for musical theatre, drama, dance, singing and tap teachers who are looking to join an award winning team. Steppin Out Stars of Tomorrow is based in Wokingham and Woodley and we look for energetic, enthusiastic and passionate teachers who are qualified or who are at drama or dance school and in their second year, or above.

Contact Shelley on 07970 034488

Shelley@steppinoutstars.co.uk

Theatrebugs

Theatrebugs is always on the lookout for enthusiastic drama teachers in London and the Home Counties who have a natural affinity with young children (Under 5s)! Theatrebugs prides itself on instilling confidence and creativity in a manner that is fun and entertaining. Therefore we are looking for bubbly, energetic individuals who can develop a kind, caring and patient relationship with the children and nursery school staff alike. Excellent communication skills are essential.

If this sounds like you, we would love to hear from you! We offer a range of exciting opportunities for our teachers, from running regular classes, to leading holiday workshops and touring Christmas pantomimes. Teachers will receive full training, ongoing support and complete class plans as well as excellent rates of pay.

Full, clean driving license, a car, and teaching experience are useful but not essential. You must possess an up to date clean enhanced DBS in order to work for us, this can be processed through us if you do not yet have one. Theatrebugs is committed to safeguarding and promoting the welfare of children and young people and expects all staff and volunteers to share this commitment. Drop us an email to recruitment@theatrebugs.co.uk and check us out here: *www.theatrebugs.co.uk*

Theatrebugs currently operates in hundreds of venues:

Throughout London and Greater London

Epsom and surrounding areas

Bedford and surrounding areas

Guildford and surrounding areas

West Oxfordshire Academy Of Performing Arts (WOAPA)

WOAPA is an award winning independent theatre school for children aged 4-16 years, which operates in Witney Oxfordshire at weekends, during the standard academic term. Our classes are led by experienced and enthusiastic tutors whose skills in working with young people will enable children to develop at their own pace, and encourage them to reach their true potential. We have an ongoing recruitment system—tutors can apply to us at any time, and if they fit our criteria, we keep their details on file and contact them when we are looking for a tutor. After initial contact, I respond to all applicants, requesting they send me their CV. I do make it clear that I look for tutors who are in for the duration—not someone who is going to be around for a short time. Please contact brian@woapa.co.uk.

www.woapa.co.uk

The Young Actors Company

We have been teaching and training children and young people in the arts for over 40 years. We recruit professionally trained, highly skilled and experienced actors and directors. Please send your CVs to info@theyoungactorscompany.com.

www.theyoungactorscompany.com

Cambridge	London (Notting Hill)
Peterborough	Birmingham
Colchester	

THE INTERVIEW

Ellie Tillotson, Freelance Drama Teacher

Which companies do you currently work for as a freelance drama teacher?

Carney Academy, Hoot Creative Arts, Artlink West Yorkshire, and Upstage Youth Theatre

Which companies have you worked for in the past?

Grimm and Co, Door84 Youth Centre, ACT Academy and ICU Transformational Arts

Did you go to university or drama school, and if so which one and what did you study?

I studied at the Royal Central School of Speech and Drama, on the Drama, Applied Theatre and Education course.

How did you get your first job as a drama teacher?

I did lots of research into local organisations, charities and drama schools, and contacted them directly. Lots of organisations have a pool of freelancers that they work with, and if you can become part of their network you will often find a steady stream of work coming through. I attended lots of networking events to meet new people and arts organisations; these events gave me lots of new contacts and ongoing support. I also got in touch with local practitioners and teachers: hearing about people's first-hand experience was invaluable.

What advice would you give to someone who wants to be a freelance drama teacher?

Do your research, know your aim and be prepared. I found that having some savings before I got started was a huge help: it takes the pressure off and allows you to seek work that is relevant to your skillset and interests. Set up a professional profile on social media sites and consider building a website. My website allows me to document my work, advertise projects and provide potential clients with a visual CV to flick though. It's also really important to know the legal and financial implications of freelancing, from taxes to insurance. Be a professional from the outset and have high expectations of yourself.

What's your favourite drama game?

Catch phrases. This was introduced to me by a group of students and it is absolutely hilarious. It's a great way of establishing high energy, identifying projection and voice as well as encouraging groups to be silly and playful! You start by setting a theme: this game can be done through lots of different genres or themes such as fairy tales, EastEnders, American Slang and Wild West.

Each participant picks a phrase and an action for the given theme, for example if we were doing Wild West, it might be 'I got a snake in my boots!' or 'This town ain't big enough for the two of us.' Once each participant has their own phrase and an action, go around the circle to recap each one (participants need to remember each phrase). The teacher starts with his or her phrase and action, and then performs someone else's catch phrase in the circle. Whoever's phrase was picked by the teacher, must then perform their phrase and action for the group, followed by someone else's in the circle, and so on. If a participant freezes, pauses or laughs - they are out of the game!

What's your teaching philosophy in a nutshell?

Be brave, trust your instincts and have fun!

The Silver and Gold Packages

This book is also available as part of a larger, silver package containing:

- Thirty-five ready-to-print scenes for performance and classroom use adapted from classics including *The Railway Children, Little Red Riding Hood, Oliver Twist, A Little Princess, Wind and the Willows, Little Women, Snow White, The Wonderful Wizard of Oz, The Secret Garden, Animal Farm, Jane Eyre, Great Expectations* and *Pride and Prejudice*

- Fully licensed scripts for *Alice in Wonderland* adapted for 3-7-year olds, 7-11-year-olds and 11-21-year-olds

- A fully licensed musical score for each *Alice in Wonderland* adaptation, ready to transfer to your iPod or burn to CD and use for public performances.

The gold package also contains these, plus individual coaching from the author as you develop your career as a freelance drama teacher.

If you've already bought this book, you can get a discount on these packages by visiting

dramafountain.com/upgrade